The Ultimate American Football Trivia Book

An Amazing Collection with Over 700 Trivia Questions, Stories, and Fun Facts for NFL Fans

D1607462

Brainy Tiger

BONUS

Because we always like to *give more*, now we have a *BONUS* for you:

BONUS <u>**The Top Ten Rules Of The Greatest Champions And The Most Successful People On The Planet**</u>, in **PDF** version.

Claim your *BONUS* by sending us an email at <u>TheBrainyTiger@Gmail.com</u> and telling us the name of the book you purchased, and we will be happy to send you this fantastic *BONUS*

TABLE OF CONTENTS

AN INTRODUCTION

On a cold winter day in 1988, in a small town in New York, I sat freezing in my local high school's football stands. My band uniform was not nearly warm enough to keep out the wind, but there I sat dutifully, waiting for the clock to countdown to halftime. That is when the uniformed players would leave the field, and the marching band would take it, perform for two minutes, and march off.

Well, I thought, if I have to *be* here for every home game, I may as well learn about football.

So began a love affair with football that has lasted over 30 years.

The concept seemed so simple at; first it was like the marching band's choreography at halftime.

Essentially, it all boiled down to this:

Each team had four chances to move the ball ten yards.

That was it; that's how it worked. If the team successfully moved the ball ten yards with four chances, they had the opportunity to do it again and again until they crossed the magical end zone to score six points. If they failed, they had to give the other team the same four chances to move the ball ten yards towards their end zone.

It seemed easy enough to follow at first. Teams seemed to either throw (pass) or ran with the football to 'pick up' yards.

That same marching band student learned the plays' names, the titles of the players' positions, and eventually, the coaches. NFL history, the trades, the rivalries, the behind-the-scenes stories (why did the New England Patriots yell "BOO!" to the New York Jets, but not the New York Giants? When did the Los Angeles Rams move to St. Louis, Missouri, and why? And then move back to Los Angeles again? Who picks the colors of the uniforms? (I became just as interesting as watching the games for the colors and teams' backgrounds as hearing about the scores and the standings). And what was Fantasy Football?

About ten years later, sitting in the hectic lunch hour rush of the ESPN ZONE restaurant in New York City, that same high school girl, now a college graduate was eating with her mother. The servers asked trivia questions to all the tables around them, but none were coming their way. Confident that I knew my football, I exclaimed, "I wonder why we aren't getting any sports trivia questions"...the waiter spun around and calmly stated, "Deion Sanders has played major league football and baseball for eight different teams.

Name them."

"The Dallas Cowboys," I replied. It with the most obvious answer. "I'll need a minute to get back to you on the rest."

All those years later, the most straightforward trivia question was overwhelming.

So....what is football all about?

There are so many facets to the sport of football--even when narrowed to the NFL.

College, fantasy, high school football--they have their myths, legends, and history.   But the NFL is the crowning jewel of American sports. A myriad of award-winning movies, both based in fact and fiction, have been produced on the subject, ranging from the silly and super "The Replacements" to the serious and somber "Concussion." To summarize the regard with which Americans hold NFL football, I offer a paraphrase from the movie Concussion: a doctor wants to sue the NFL for withholding information on head trauma; another doctor tells him he is crazy.

 "You want to go up against a national sports league that practically owns a day of the week?! AND, that day was formerly owned by the CHURCH!"

Further, the residents of Green Bay, Wisconsin, are actually shareholders of the corporation that is Green Bay Packers football. The Pittsburgh Steelers claim they "Bleed black and yellow," their team colors. When the Buffalo Bills lost four Super Bowls in a row in the early 1990s, the market value of homes in that city actually dropped.

True football fans take the sport so seriously they paint their homes in team colors, name their child after a favorite player, or plan their weeks around game times. They observe superstitions, learn chants and histories, and bond with otherwise perfect strangers. The National Football League is in the DNA of most Americans.

NFL History

1. What does the NFL stand for?

   a. National Football League   b. National Federal League

   c. Named Football League

2. In what year was the NFL founded?

   a. 1900   b. 1910   c. 1920

3. What was the NFL called before it was the NFL?

   a. The Football League b. All-America Football Association

       c. American Football Company

4. How many teams existed when the NFL was founded?

   a. 8   b. 6   c. 10

5. How many states were represented when the NFL was founded?

   a. 4   b. 5   c. 6

6. What is the oldest, still functioning NFL team?

   a. Miami Dolphins b. New York Giants   c. Green Bay Packers

7. Who was the first NFL President?

   a. Dan Marino   b. Red Grange   c. Jim Thorpe

8. Who wrote the rules of football?

   a. Walter Camp   b. Mike Naismith   c. Bob Hope

9. How many rules existed when football was founded (with subsections)?

   a. 4   b. 5   c. 6

10. What American university has a football stadium named for the founder of football?

    a. Huron College b. Yale University c. Carson College

Answers: 1-a, 2-c, 3-b, 4-a, 5-a, 6-c, 7-c, 8-a, 9-b, 10-b

11. Who was the first player paid to play football ($500)?

    a. William Heffelfinger   b. Jim Thorpe c. Paddy Driscoll

12. When was the first 'championship' game played in the NFL?

    a. 1923 b. 1933 c. 1943

13. Which two teams played in the first championship game?

    a. Portsmouth Spartans and Chicago Bears b. Chicago Bears and Green Bay Packers c. New York Jets and New York Giants

14. In what year did the NFL split into two divisions?

    a. 1933 b. 1935 c.1937

15. In 1942, when the Pittsburgh Steelers and Philadelphia Eagles merged for the season, what was their name?

    a. Eaglers b. SteelersEagles c. Steagles

16. Who won the NFL Championship Game in 1944?

    a. Green Bay Packers b. Arizona Cardinals c. Kansas City Chiefs

17. In what year did whistles replace horns on the field?

    a. 1942 b. 1944 c. 1948

18. Which Native American, of Sauk descent, was both an Olympic decathlon athlete and professional baseball player before becoming an NFL player?

    a. Walter Camp b. Red Grange c. Jim Thorpe

19. What competitor football league formed in 1946 to challenge the NFL, but ultimately went out of business?

    a. The All-America Football Conference b. The Better Football League c. The US Football League

20. How many states were represented when the NFL was founded?

    a. 4 b. 6 c. 8

Answers: 11-a, 12-b, 13-b, 14-a, 15-c, 16-a, 17-b, 18-c, 19-a, 20-c

21. Instead of coming up with original names for their teams, new NFL teams based their names on what other sports team names?

a. Baseball   b. Basketball   c. Lacrosse

22. Before there was an official Super Bowl, how did the NFL crown its 'champion?'

a. vote   b. choose a name out of a hat   c. win loss record

23. In what year did the NFL draft start?

a. 1936   b. 1946   c. 1956

24. In what year did the competing American Football League join the NFL?

a. 1960   b. 1970   c. 1980

25. In what year did a woman first officiate an NFL game?

a. 1992   b. 2002   c. 2012

26. Which football fixture personally picked an All American Team from 1889-1924?

a. Walter Camp   b. Grantland Rice   c. Joel Whitacker

27. What Marvel actor is a fan of the Atlanta Falcons?

a. Mark Ruffalo   b. Robert Downey Jr.   c. Samuel L. Jackson

28. Which NFL quarterback won the Heismann, the O'Brien, the Maxwell, and the Walter Camp Awards, and was the top draft pick?

a. Brett Favre   b. Drew Brees   c. Vinny Testeverde

29. What day of the week has NOT had an NFL game?

a. Friday   b. Wednesday   c. NFL games have been played on all days

30. In what year were college juniors first allowed in the NFL draft?

a. 1970   b. 1980   c. 1990

Answers: 21-a, 22-c, 23-a, 24-b, 25-c, 26-a, 27-c, 28-c, 29-c, 30-c

DID YOU KNOW?

1. Sleeves on NFL jerseys cannot be torn or cut.

2. The NFL logo must appear on the jersey, pants, and helmets of all players.

3. All players must wear white stockings on their legs from their ankles to the bottom of their pants, leaving no skin exposed.

4. Three teams in the NFL have never re-designed their jerseys: New Orleans Saints, Indianapolis Colts, and Cleveland Browns.

5. More than 90% of NFL quarterbacks are right-handed.

6. Because of time zones and television ratings, 1pm games on the east coast of the United States begin at 10am on the west coast.

7. The oldest player to kick a Point After Kick was *not* a kicker, it was a quarterback named Doug Flutie.

8. The oldest player to have a 400+ yard passing game was Brett Favre, at 41 years old.

9. Rod Woodson holds the record for the most interceptions returned for a touchdown in the course of his career.

10. Until 1943, players were not required to wear a helmet during play.

"Today I will do what others won't, so tomorrow I can accomplish what others can't." – Jerry Rice

II. The Football Field

1. What are the dimensions of the NFL football field?

    a.   360ft x 160ft   b. 300ft x100ft   c. 350ft x 200ft

2. How deep are the End Zones?

    a.   20 yards   b. 10 yards   c. 5 yards

3. When were the field dimensions established?

    a.   1875   b. 1879   c.1881

4. How often do Yard Lines appear on the field?

    a.   Every 5 yards   b. Every 10 yards   c. Every 20 yards

5. What is the centerline of the football field called?

    a.   Mid Field   b. Half Yard Point   c. 50 Yard Line

6. How often do numbers appear on the football field?

    a.   Every 10 yards   b. Every 5 yards   c. Every yard

7. What is the name of the lines that run parallel to sidelines at 70 feet, 9 inches, for the entire length of the football field?

    a.   Hash Marks   b. Mid Field Marks   c. Placement Marks

8. When is an NFL player 'out of bounds?'

    a.   When his arms leave the field   b. When one foot touches the sidelines of the football field   c. When his body crosses the sidelines the field

9. Who are the only people not allowed on the player benches behind the field?

    a.   Players b. Doctors C. Security

10. What does the expression "splitting the uprights" mean?

    a.   Standing between the quarterback and linesmen   b. Running through the defensive line c. Kicking the ball through the goalposts

Answer: 1-a, 2-b, 3-c, 4-b, 5-c, 6-1, 7-a, 8-b, 9-c, 10-c

DID YOU KNOW?

1. Super Bowl Sunday sees record lows in the number of marriages performed.

2. Gale Sayers was the youngest player to be inducted into the Football Hall of Fame at the age of 34.

3. Brett Favre's first pass completion was to himself.

4. The oldest person in the Football Hall of Fame is Ed Sabol, the founder of NFL Films. He was 99 at the time of his death.

5. The team with the highest number of retired jerseys is the Chicago Bears.

6. The first professional African American football player was Charles Follis, and he played in 1904.

7. Green Bay, Wisconsin is known as "Title Town," for their early winning streak in NFL history.

8. Until the 1960 NFL season, all players were expected to play on both the offense and the defense; this was known as Ironman Style.

9. The Minnesota Vikings have never won a Super Bowl.

10. The Lombardi Trophy is made of Sterling Silver and cost $25,000 to create.

"**Treat a person as he is, and he will remain as he is. Treat him as he could be, and he will become what he should be.**" – Jimmy Johnson

III. The Equipment, the Uniform, and Penalties

1. On an NFL jersey, which position normally wears a number between 1-19?

    a.   Running backs b. Punters c. Quarterbacks

2. What is another name for the face mask that is attached to the player's helmet?

    a.   Cage b. unit c. shield

3. How many players are allowed on the field at a time?

    a.   15/team b. 13/team c. 11/team

4. What are the two groups on the field called?

    a.   Right and Left b. Offense and Defense c. Dark and Light

5. Who receives the ball on the opening kickoff?

    a.   The winner of the coin toss b. The home team c. The visiting team

6. What does the phrase 'three and out' mean?

    a.   Three yards and the quarter is over b. three players are injured c. three tries for a first down failed

7. How many points is a touchdown worth?

    a.   6   b. 7   c. 8

8. How many ways can a team try for extra points after a touchdown?

    a.   1   b. 2   c. 3

9. In what year was the two-point conversion officially added to the NFL?

    a.   1974   b. 1984   c. 1994

10. How many points is a field goal worth?

    a.   1   b. 3   c. 5

Answers: 1-c, 2-a, 3-c, 4-b, 5-a, 6-c, 7-a, 8-b, 9-c, 10-b

11. How many points is a safety worth?

    a. 1   b. 2   c. 3

12. What is an infraction of the rules called?

    a. Penalty   b. Mistake   c. Yellow Card

13. Which official has the final judgement in a disagreement on the field?

    a. Referee   b. Captain   c. Visiting Coach

14. Which official watches the line of scrimmage (where play begins)?

    a. Umpire   b. Medical Trainer   c. Line Judge

15. On which side of the ball does the umpire stand?

    a. Defensive side b. Offensive side c. The ump switches sides

16. Which official is in charge of the play clock?

    a. Line Judge   b. Clock Judge c. Head Coach

17. When an official signals with his arm making a large circle in front of himself, what is he saying?

    a. Keep playing b. Clock doesn't stop c. Game over

18. What is the name for the penalty resulting from a player entering the neutral zone and making contact with an opponent before the ball is snapped?

    a. Encroachment b. Off Sides   c. Delay

19. What penalty occurs when a player receives a kick and is helpless of prone, yet opposing members jump onto his body?

    a. Mountain-ing   b. Spearing   c. Piling On

20. Hitting a defenseless receiver is which penalty?

    a. Unnecessary roughness b. Clipping   c. Holding

Answers: 11-b, 12-a, 13-a, 14-a, 15-a, 16-a, 17-b, 18-a, 19-c, 20-a

21. What penalty is signaled when the referee moves his right open palm forward from his shoulder?

    a. illegal formation   b. illegal receiver c. illegal contact

22. What penalty is signaled when the referee folds his arms across his chest?

    a. holding b. interference c. delay of game

23. What penalty is signaled when the referee pulls his bent fingers in a downward motion over his face?

    a. facemask   b. unsportsmanlike conduct   c. holding

24. What penalty is signaled when the referee places his hands on his hips?

    a. off sides   b. encroachment   c. intentional grounding

25. What penalty is being signaled when the referee places his hands on his head?

    a. false start   b. interference   c. illegal substitution

26. What penalty is being signaled when the referee places the palms of his hands behind his head?

    a. interference   b. loss of down   c. fumble

27. What penalty is the referee signaling when he sticks his thumb out and points behind himself?

    a. false start   b. ejection   c. incomplete pass

28. When a referee grabs a closed fist around the wrist with one hand, what penalty is he signaling?

    a. clipping   b. holding   c. spearing

29. When a referee rotates arms over each other, what is he signaling?

    a. False start   b. encroachment   c. off sides

30. What is the NFL record for penalties in one game?

    a. 22   b. 24   c. 26

Answers: 21-c, 22-c, 23-a, 24-a, 25-c, 26-b, 27-b, 28-b, 29-a, 30-c

31. Where do players NOT wear pads?

    a. feet   b. shoulders c. thighs

32. What is the name of the pads that protect the rib cage?

    a. rib pads   b. flak jacket   c. trunk pads

33. How many different lengths of cleats are there?

    a. 2   b. 3 c. 4

34. What disqualifies tape on an NFL uniform?

    a. it is clear   b. it matches the team colors   c. it is an inch long

35. What color jersey does the visiting team usually wear?

    a. white with trim b. the darkest team color c. depends on the day

36. What must appear on all players' shoes?

    a. NFL logo   b. team name c. division name

37. What penalty is the referee signaling when he moves his palms up and down in front of his body?

    a. illegal substitution   b. juggled pass   c. out of bounds

38. What is the referee signaling when he waves his arms above his head?

    a. timeout   b. off sides c. intentional grounding

39. How many yards are charged when a team has an encroachment penalty?

    a. 15 yards   b. 10 yards   c. 5 yards

40. If a player trips another player, what is the penalty?

    a. 15 yards   b. 10 yards   c. 5 yards

Answers: 31-a, 32-b, 33-c, 34-c, 35-a, 36-a, 37-b, 38-a, 39-c, 40-b

DID YOU KNOW?

1. 31 of 32 NFL teams have cheerleaders--only the Pittsburgh Steelers do not have them.
2. Steve Young is the only left hander in the Football Hall of Fame.
3. More than 100 million people watch the Super Bowl every year.
4. In 1906 President Theodore Roosevelt introduced the forward pass to the game.
5. ALL NFL footballs are made in Ada, Ohio, at the Wilson factory.
6. The Baltimore Ravens are not named after the bird. The team is named after the Edgar Allan Poe poem, "The Raven," because Poe was from Baltimore.
7. In 2011, advertisers paid $3 million for a 30 second commercial during the Super Bowl.
8. Future Football Hall of Famer Johnny Unitas was cut as a fourth string quarterback by the Pittsburgh Steelers before being signed by one of their biggest rivals, the Baltimore Ravens.
9. In the 1930s, Eagles team owner Bert Bell proposed the idea of a football draft to help 'spread the wealth' of players coming out of college, who were consistently signing with the top four teams.
10. The Pittsburgh Steelers first draft pick ever was a player from Notre Dame University named William Shakespeare. Shakespeare never played however, deciding to enter the business world instead.

"**Football is like life – it requires perseverance, self-denial, hard work, sacrifice, dedication and respect for authority.**" – Vince Lombardi

IV. The Quarterback and Offensive Line (The General and his O Line)

1. Who does the Quarterback line up behind on every play?

   a. The Running Back   b. The Center   c. The Safety

2. How does the Quarterback communicate with the coaches during play?

   a. Hand signs   b. Messages   c. Audio Unit in Helmet

3. What is the area where the quarterback operates called?

   a. The Zone   b. The Play   c. The Pocket

4. What is a Quarterback Sneak?

   a. The quarterback runs with the ball b. The quarterback runs off the field

   c. The quarterback doesn't play

5. Normally, the Quarterback will throw or do what with the ball?

   a. Run   b. Toss backwards   c. Punt

6. When a Quarterback calls an 'audible,' what does that mean?

   a. the quarterback is changing the coach's play b. the quarterback is calling for a time out   c. the quarterback is name calling

7. How fast can a good Quarterback through a football?

   a. 45-50 mph   b. 55-60mph   c. 65-70mph

8. Roughly how many passing plays does a Quarterback need to know?

   a. 150   b. 200   c. 250

9. Roughly how many running plays does a Quarterback need to know?

   a. 50   b. 60   c. 70

10. What is the football term used when a Quarterback moves backwards while holding the football?

a. backing   b. surrendering   c. retreating

Answers: 1-b, 2-c, 3-c, 4-a, 5-a, 6-a, 7-a, 8-b, 9-a, 10-c

11. Which quarterback was a surprise success coming out of the University of Michigan?

    a. Otto Graham   b. Tom Brady   c. Joe Montana

12. Which great NFL quarter back retired after two Super Bowl wins?

    a. Drew Brees   b. Peyton Manning   c. John Elway

13. Who is the only Cleveland Browns quarterback to lead the team to ten 'Championship Games' (the precursor to the Super Bowl)?

    a. Baker Mayfield b. Brady Quinn c. Otto Graham

14. Which NFL quarterback was rarely sacked because he was so quick on his release?

    a. Dan Marino   b. Steve Young   c. Walter Moon

15. Who was the #1 overall pick in the 1998 NFL draft?

    a. Eli Manning   b. Peyton Manning   c. Tom Brady

16. Who is the only quarterback named Super Bowl MVP three times?

    a. Tom Brady   b. Dan Marino c. Joe Montana

17. Which NFL quarterback has the highest QB rating at 96.8%?

    a. Tom Brady   b. Steve Young c. Peyton Manning

18. Whose quarterback records remain in the top ten 40 years after his retirement?

    a. Fran Tarkenton   b. Terry Bradshaw   c. Joe Montana

19. Which NFL quarterback won the Super Bowl for the Colts in 1970?

    a. Otto Graham   b. John Harbaugh   c. Johnny Unitas

20. Who was the quarterback on the "Immaculate Reception" play?

    a. Howie Long   b. Terry Bradshaw   c. Steve Young

Answers: 11-b, 12-c, 13-c, 14-b, 15-b, 16-c, 17-b, 18-a, 19-c, 20-b

DID YOU KNOW?

1. Almost 78% of NFL players file for bankruptcy within two years of leaving the game.
2. Only one professional athlete has played in both a Superbowl and a World series—Deion Sanders (with the Atlanta Falcons and the Atlanta Braves).
3. From 1947 to 1998, the Arizona Cardinals lost every post season game.
4. The Chicago Bears have more retired umbers than any other NFL team; some teams do not officially retire any jersey numbers.
5. There is only about 11 minutes of actual playing time in an NFL game.
6. The huddle was invented by a Deaf quarterback named Paul Hubbard, so opposing teams could not see him signing to his teammates.
7. There is only one left-handed quarterback in the Football Hall of Fame, Steve Young.
8. NFL cancelled its full week of upcoming games the week after the 9/11 disaster.
9. There have been 217 father/son pairs in the NFL.
10. As of 2021, the only women allowed on the field during play are referees.

"You're never a loser until you quit trying" – Mike Ditka

V. The Running Game and Passing Game

1. What is the stance for a running back?

   a. two-point stance   b. three-point stance   c. four-point stance

2. What is a handoff?

   a. quarterback hands the ball to the running back

   b. quarterback kicks away

   c. quarterback throws the ball

3. What is the job of the full back?

   a. throw the football   b. handoff the football   c. block the receivers

4. How many running plays are in a typical NFL playbook?

   a. 25-50   b. 50-100   c. 100-150

5. What is the running back's top priority?

   a. making the touchdown   b. protecting the football   c. passing the ball

6. What is a deflection?

   a. a fake out play

   b. a defender touching the ball to move it away from the receiver

   c. an interception

7. What is a sack?

   a. dropping the football b. a fumble

   c. tackling the quarterback behind the line of scrimmage

8. What is another name for a pass pattern?

   a. a pass route   b. a pass routine   c. a pass try

9. What is the name of the pass 8-12 yards beyond the line of scrimmage?

   a. hook   b. curl   c. slant

10. What is a simple throw to the running back towards the sideline?

    a. swing   b. hook   c. slant

Answers: 1-a, 2-a, 3-c, 4-b, 5-b, 6-b, 7-c, 8-a, 9-b, 10-a

11. Which offensive position is considered the most physically demanding position?

    a. running back   b. wide receiver c. safety

12. Which offensive player protects the halfback?

    a. running back   b. full back   c. wide receiver

13. What is another name for the two-point stance?

    a. leg stance   b. ready stance   c. up stance

14. What is the name of the play when the quarterback tosses the ball to the full back?

    a. pitch   b. tug toss   c. flip flop

15. What is the name of the offensive play where the team slides to the right?

    a. slide   b. veer   c. cross

16. What is another name for the left tackle position?

    a. strong side   b. blind side   c. left side

17. Which offensive player has to know the signal count?

    a. quarterback   b. left tackle   c. center

18. Which offensive player snaps the football to the quarterback?

    a. center   b. right tackle c. left tackle

19. What is the play: two offense linesmen blocking one defenseman?

    a. two on one   b. double trouble   c. double team

20. What is the play: the offense defends an area of the field?

    a. zone block   b. space block   c. yard block

Answers: 11-a, 12-b, 13-c, 14-a, 15-b, 16-b, 17-c, 18-a, 19-c, 20-a

DID YOU KNOW?

1. Every year since 2002 a team has gone from worst to first in its division.

2. The New England Patriots were the first team to purchase their own airplanes to travel to away games.

3. Wilson the only company permitted to make NFL footballs, produces 4,000 footballs a day.

4. There are 16 lace holes on an NFL football, but only one single lace.

5. The Dallas Cowboys season records are 8-8 for 2011, 2012, and 2013.

6. NFL cheerleaders are paid ess than $100 per game.

7. Legendary NFL quarterback Brett Favre's first attempted pass was an interception, and resulted in a touchdown for the opposing team.

8. The Chicago Bears "Superbowl Shuffle" was nominated for a Grammy Award in 1987.

9. Detroit Lions kicker Harvard Rugland reports that he learned English by listening to the rap group Wu Tang Clan.

10. Since 1999, the Cleveland Browns have used a league high of over 20 quarterbacks, and only 2 have had winning records.

"I never left the field saying I could have done more to get ready and that gives me piece of mind." – Peyton Manning

VI. The Defensive Line (The D Line)

1. What is the goal of the defensive line on a running play?

   a. tackle the quarterback   b. tackle the ball carrier   c. score

2. What is the goal of the defensive line on a passing play?

   a. tackle the quarterback   b. tackle the ball carrier   c. score

3. Which NFL team is known to have the best defense of all time?

   a. 1985 Chicago Bears   b. 1992 Buffalo Bills   c. 1995 New York Jets

4. Which NFL defensive player has the most sacks?

   a. Julius Peppers   b. Reggie White   c. Bruce Smith

5. Which NFL defensive player majored in classical music in college an quit football after five seasons with the Bengals to become a Grammy award winning songwriter?

   a. Mike Reid   b. Chris Doleman   c. Kevin Greene

6. Which defensive player is typically the fastest?

   a. linesman   b. cornerback   c. free safety

7. Which Pro Football Hall of Fame player had 71 interceptions in his career?

   a. Ron Woodson   b. Darren Sharper   c. Dave Brown

8. Which safety positions himself 12-15 yards behind the line of scrimmage?

   a. strong safety   b. free safety   c. dime safety

9. What is the name a tackle from the feet of a jumping receiver?

   a. groundhog tackle   b. toe tickler   c. toe tackle

10. What is the ultimate goal of the defense?

   a. score   b. force a turnover   c. sack the quarterback

Answers: 1-b, 2-a, 3-a, 4-b, 5-a, 6-b, 7-a, 8-b, 9-a, 10-b

11. Which stance do the defensive linesman use?

    a. two-point stance   b. three-point stance c. four-point stance

12. What is the name of the defensive player who lines up with the center?

    a. the main defender b. the defense center   c. the nose tackle

13. Which linebacker lines up across from the tight end?

    a. the Sam   b. the Lou   c. the Pete

14. What is a hurry?

    a. defenders forcing the throw b. jumping before the snap

    c. committing a penalty

15. What is the term for defensive players moving around after they seem to be settled on the line?

    a. twitching   b. stemming   c. grooving

16. What is the name for the statistic of passes deflected by defenders?

    a. pass stat   b. deflect stat   c. pass defensed

17. What is the term for a pass caught by a defender?

    a. fumble   b. interception   c. interference

18. Safeties, cornerbacks, and 'nickelbacks' are part of which line?

    a. D line   b. O line   c. Special Teams

19. What is the main job of the defensive end?

    a. intercept the football b. rush the quarterback c. force a pass

20. Who is widely considered to be the greatest linebacker of all time?

    a. Jack Hamm b. Chuck Bednarik   c. Dick Butkus

Answers: 11-b, 12-c, 13-a, 14-a, 15-b, 16-c, 17-b, 18-a, 19-c, 20-c

DID YOU KNOW?

1. The waiting list for season tickets to the Green Bay Packers is almost 1,000 years. 1,000.
2. The oldest NFL record is from 1929: Ernie Nevers scored 40 points in one game, getting six touchdowns and four points after.
3. Walter Payton broke OJ Simpson's rushing record on November 20, 1977—while he was also battling a high fever, chills, and the flu.
4. The actor Carl Weathers, who played Apollo Creed in the Rocky movies, played for two seasons with the Oakland Raiders.
5. The New York Jets have never beaten the Philadelphia Eagles.
6. NFL rules state that no stadium may be built facing North/South, so neither team will have the sun in its players' eyes for any amount of time.
7. During the 1957 NFL Championship Game (what eventually became known as the Superbowl), a television employee ran onto the field to stop play because a TV cable came loose and stopped the TV feed.
8. Lumen Field, home stadium of the Seattle Seahawks, is known as the loudest stadium in the world. This is the result of the architectural design increasing crowd noise.
9. The Seattle Seahawks refer to the fans as "The 12th Man."
10.   Commercials make up 60 minutes of a three-hour football broadcast.

"If what you did YESTERDAY seems big, you haven't done anything TODAY."-- Lou Holtz

VII. The Kickers and the Punters

1. As of 2020, which kicker holds the record for longest field goal?

     a. Tom Dempsey   b. Adam Vinatieri   c. Chris Boswell

2. As of 2020, which kickers holds the record for most field goals completed?

     a. Chris Boswell   b. John Carney   c. Adam Vinatieri

3. How many kickers are in the NFL Hall of Fame?

     a. 1   b. 5   c. 10

4. How many kickers have been named MVP of a Superbowl?

     a. 0   b. 5   c.10

5. Who was the first punter to be drafted in the first round of the NFL draft?

     a. Sam Martin   b. Nsimba Webster   c. William Ray Guy

6. Who was the first African American Punter in the NFL?

     a. Reggie Robbie   b. Marquette King   c. Greg Coleman

7. Which part of the football team does the punter play for?

     a. offense   b. defense   c. special teams

8. How many pure punters are in the Pro Football Hall of Fame?

     a. 1   b. 4   c. 10

9. Out of the 32 NFL teams, how many punters use their left foot exclusively?

     a. 10   b. 16   c. 22

10. Which position often doubles for the punter?

     a. backup quarterback   b. linesman   c. running back

Answers: 1-a, 2-c, 3-1, 4-a, 5-c, 6-c, 7-c, 8-a, 9-c, 10-a

11. What is the term for a punted ball that reaches the end zone?

    a. dead ball   b. down ball   c. touchback

12. Who is the punter of the Raiders who was drafted in the first round of the 1973 NFL draft?

    a. Adam Vinitieri   b. Ray Guy   c. Matt Stover

13. What is the average yardage of a punt return?

    a. 8 yards   b. 20 yards   c. 30 yards

14. What can college punters do that NFL punters cannot?

    a. a one-inch ball support   b. ankle braces   c. a stopwatch

15. How far behind the ball does the kicking team line up?

    a. 5 yards   b. 10 yards   c. 15 yards

16. What signal keeps the kicking team away from the receiver?

    a. fair catch   b. stop the clock   c. fair game

17. Where is the ball placed if it goes out of bounds?

    a. their own 40-yard line   b. 50-yard line   c. where the ball went out

18. What is a percentage kick?

    a. a high kick   b. a long kick   c. a low kick with a bounce

19. What is the term for a trying to kick to a certain side of the field?

    a. directional kicking   b. trick kicking   c. high kicking

20. What was the special term Jimmy Johnson had for returned yards from a kick?

    a. hidden yards b. special yards c. extra yards

Answers: 11-c, 12-b, 13-a, 14-a, 15-c, 16-a, 17-a, 18-c, 19-a, 20-a

DID YOU KNOW?

1. The New England Patriots were almost called the Bay State Patriots, after the nickname for the state of Massachusetts.
2. One NFL player has died on the field; Chuck Hughes of the Detroit Lions was 28 and had a heart attack while playing against the Chicago Bears in 1971.
3. Football is based on the combination of soccer and rugby.
4. Between 1995 and 2015, Los Angeles, the second largest television market in America, did not have an NFL team.
5. Some teams that once existed in the NFL were the Maroons, the Yellowjackets, the Americans, and the Celts.
6. President Theodore Roosevelt was so concerned with the safety of NFL payers he threatened to ban the game if it did not create rules to keep players safe.
7. Officially, the shape of a football is a 'prolate spheroid.'
8. All NFL footballs must be inscribed with the initials "NFL" and the stamped signature of the NFL Commissioner.
9. College footballs and NFL footballs differ in one significant way; college footballs have white stripes on each end, making them easier to see.
10. Alan Page was the first defensive NFL player to win an MVP award; he later went on to become a Mississippi Supreme Court Justice.

"If you aren't going all the way, why go at all?" – Joe
Namath

VIII. Team Histories

1. What name was The Washington Football Team formerly known as?

    a. Boston Braves   b. Washington Senators   c. Washington Caps

2. How much money did owner Dan Snyder spend on the Washington Team?

    a. $200m   b. $500m   c. $800m

3. In what year did the Washington Football Team officially adopt that name?

    a. 2008   b, 2017   c.2021

4. During the 1987 NFL strike, the Washington Football Team (known at the time as the Redskins) held what honor?

    a. none crossed the picket line   b. none went on strike   c. won every game

5. In what year did the Washington Football Team (known as the Redskins) win 11 straight games?

    a. 1981   b. 1991   c. 2001

6. In what year was The Washington Football Team founded?

    a. 1932   b. 1942   c. 1952

7. What was the nickname of the Washington Offensive line in the 1980s?

    a. The O Skins   b. The Scooters   c. The Hogs

8. What are the official colors of the Washington Football Team?

    a. Blue and White   b. Purple and Gold   c. Burgundy and Gold

9. What is the name of the Washington Football Team's home stadium?

    a. MetLife Stadium   b. Candlestick Park   c. FedEx Field

10. When was the first time the Washington Football Team (as the Redskins) won the Superbowl?

    a. 1981   b.1991   c. 2001

Answers: 1-a, 2-c, 3-c, 4-a, 5-b, 6-a, 7-c, 8-c, 9-c, 10-b

21. In what year did the New England Patriots change their name from the Boston Patriots?

    a. 1931   b. 1951   c. 1971

22. What is the name of the New England Patriots home field?

    a. Boston Stadium   b. America's Park   c. Gillette Stadium

23. What is the official fight song of the New England Patriots?

    a. I Love Boston   b. Shipping Up To Boston   c. Boston Forever

24. What are the official colors of the New England Patriots?

    a. red, white, blue   b. red, blue, yellow   c. blue, green, grey

25. What is the name of the New England Patriots mascot?

    a. Pat Patriot   b. Patriot Pete   c. Patriot Parrot

26. Who fires muskets at every Patriots games when they score?

    a. security   b. fans   c. The End Zone Militia

27. In the mid-1960s, the Patriots shared a stadium with which MLB team?

    a. New York Mets   b. New York Yankees   c. Boston Red Sox

28. Which Patriot holds the All Time Scoring record?

    a. Stephen Gostkowski   b. Tom Brady   c. Sam Cunningham

29. The Patriots played one season at which Ivy League College?

    a. Yale   b. Cornell   c. Harvard

30. Which New England Patriot claimed "I am the best decision the Patriots ever made."?

    a. Tom Brady   b. Bill Belichick   c. Randy Moss

Answers: 11-c, 12-c, 13-b, 14-a, 15-a, 16-c, 17-c, 18-a, 19-c, 20-a

21. In what year was the Buffalo Bills football team founded?

    a. 1960   b. 1970 c. 1980

22. What is the name of the Buffalo Bills team mascot?

    a. Billy Buffalo b. Billy Boy   c. Billy Bill

23. What is the Name of the Buffalo Bills Stadium?

    a. Orchard Park Stadium   b. Bills Stadium   c. New York Stadium

24. What are the colors of the Buffalo Bills uniform?

    a. grey red orange   b. red, blue, gold   c. red, white, blue

25. What four year stretch in the 1990s did the Bills win the conference, but lose the Super Bowl?

    a. 1995-1999   b. 1993-1997   c. 1990-1993

26. Who was the first Bills head coach?

    a. Jack Kemp   b. Buster Ramsey   c. Lou Saban

27. Which team represents the 'Title for NY' rivalry, as both teams play in the same division and the same state?

    a. New York Jets   b. New York Giants c. New England Patriots

28. What 'number' does the Buffalo Bills mascot wear on his jersey?

    a. 00   b. 100   c. BB

29. The Buffalo Bills had a cheerleading squad from 1967-1985. What was the squad's name?

    a. Buffalo Jills b. Buffalo Janes c. Buffalo Cuties

30. The Buffalo Bills use this classic type of halftime show, and is one of only six NFL teams to uphold this tradition, carried over from collegiate football. What it is?

    a. Marching Band b. Pop Singers   c. Audience Participation

Answers: 21-a, 22-b, 23-b, 24-c, 25-c, 26-b, 27-a, 28-c, 29-a, 30a

41. The Pittsburgh Steelers compete in which conference?

    a. AFC North   b. NFC East   c. AFC East

42. When were the Steelers founded?

    a. 1927   b.1937   c. 1947

43. What are the Steelers colors?

    a. black and silver   b. black and red   c. black and yellow

44. The Steelers share their stadium with which college football team?

    a. Penn State   b. Univ. of Penn   c. Univ. of Pittsburgh

45. What is the name of the Steelers home stadium?

    a. Heinz Field   b. Pittsburgh Stadium   c. Pennsylvania Field

46. What single family has always owned the Pittsburgh Steelers?

    a. The Rooneys   b. The Smiths   c. The Krafts

47. How many Super Bowls have the Steelers won?

    a. 2   b. 4   c. 6

48. What is the name of the yellow towel Steelers fans wave at games?

    a. Terrible Towel   b. Steelers Towel   c. Winners Towel

49. Which film featured Heinz field and several Steelers players as extras?

    a. The Dark Knight   b. The Dak Knight Rises   c. Batman Begins

50. What is the name of the Steelers mascot?

    a. Steely McBeam   b. BeamerMcSteel   c. SteelMcBeamer

Answers: 31-a, 32-a, 33-c, 34-c, 35-a, 36-a, 37-c, 38-a, 39-b, 40-a

51. How many Super Bowls have the Philadelphia Eagles won?

    a. 10   b. 5   c. 1

52. What is the Eagles fight song?

    a. Go Eagles Go   b. Fly Eagles Fly   c. Score Eagles Score

53. In what year were the Eagles formed?

    a. 1933   b. 1943   c. 1953

54. What is the name of the Eagles stadium?

    a. Eagles Field   b. Lincoln Financial Field   c. Philly Field

55. The Eagles were the subject of which Academy Award winning movie?

    a. Invincible   b. Inception   c. Intervention

56. What are the Eagles colors?

    a. blue, white, grey   b. green, white, black   c. green, yellow, grey

57. What is the Eagles nickname?

    a. The Iggles   b. The Big Birds   c. The Solo Birds

58. What conference does the Eagles play for?

    a. NFC   b. AFC   c. ABC

59. The Eagles rivalry with the Steelers is known as what?

    a. The East West Rivalry   b. North South Rivalry   c. Battle of Pennsylvania

60. What is the Eagles mascot's name?

    a. Birdie   b. Chirpers   c. Swoop

Answers: 41-1, 42-b, 43-a, 44-b, 45-a, 46-b, 47-a, 48-a, 49-c, 50-c

61. The New York Jets were established under another name in 1957; what was it?

    a.   New York Empires   b. New York Bills   c. New York Titans

62. The New York Jets play in what state?

    a.   New York   b. New Jersey c. Pennsylvania

63. What are the official colors of the New York Jets?

    a.   Green, white, black   b. green, yellow, red c. green, white, yellow

64. What is the nickname of the New York Jets?

    a.   Gang Green   b. Green Machine   c. Green Gang

65. How many times have the New York Jets won the Super Bowl?

    a.   1   b. 5   c. 10

66. What is the name of the New York Jets' home field?

    a.   New York Stadium   b. MetLife Stadium   c. Manhattan Field

67. Which NFL team do the New York Jets share their home field with?

    a.   New York Giants b. New England Patriots c. Washington Redskins

68. What is the name of the Jets Cheerleading Squad?

    a.   Jets Cheer Crew   b. Jets Flight Crew   c. Jet Girls

69. Who resigned as head coach the day he was going to be introduced by leaving a note on a napkin?

    a.   Joe Namath b. Woody Johnson   c. Bill Belichick

70. Which quarterback led the New York Jets to their only Super Bowl victory in 1968?

    a.   Mark Sanchez b. Ben Roethlisberger c. Joe Namath

Answers: 51-c, 52- b, 53-a, 54-a, 55-a, 56-b, 57-a, 58-b, 59-c, 60-c

61. In what year was the New York Giants team founded?

     a. 1925   b. 1935   c. 1945

62. How many Super Bowls have the New York Giants won?

     a. 2   b. 4   c. 6

63. What is the nickname for the New York Giants?

     a. Blue Team   b. Blue Players   c. Big Blue

64. During the 1973 football season, the New York Giants had to play at which college field?

     a. Harvard   b. Columbia   c. Yale

65. What was the name of the New York Giants first home field?

     a. Giants Stadium   b. Giants Field c. Polo Grounds

66. One of the New York Giants owners, Steve Tisch, has his name on the buildings of what local college?

     a. Columbia   b. College of New Yok City   c. New York University

67. When did the New York Giants win their first Super Bowl?

     a. 1987   b. 1977   c. 1967

68. What are the official team colors of the New York Giants?

     a. red, white, blue   b. orange, white, blue   c. red, yellow, blue

69. What division is the New York Giants team a part of?

     a. AFC east   b. NFC east   c. NFC north

70. Which New York Giants receiver had a one-handed catch named after him?

     a. Odell Beckham, Jr.   b. Eli Manning c. Frank Gifford

Answers: 61-a, 62-b, 63-c, 64-c, 65-c, 66-c, 67-a, 68-a, 69-b, 70-a

71. What are the official colors of the Baltimore Ravens?

   a. black and gold   b. black and purple   c. black and silver

72. The Baltimore Ravens were named after a poem by which author?

   a. William Shakespeare   b. Emily Dickenson   c. Edgar Allen Poe

73. Baltimore had an NFL team that left the city; when did the Ravens return?

   a. 1986   b. 1996   c. 2006

74. Which conference is the Baltimore Ravens a part of?

   a. AFC North   b. NFC North   c. AFC East

75. How many Super Bowls have the Baltimore Ravens won?

   a. 8   b. 5   c. 2

76. What is the name of the Baltimore Ravens home stadium?

   a. M&T Bank Stadium   b. Chase Bank Stadium c. MD Bank Stadium

77. Which Baltimore Ravens quarterback has had 300+ passing yards in both a regular season and post season games?

   a. Johnny Unitas   b. Joe Flacco   c. Kyle Boller

78. What is the traditional halftime entertainment offered by the Baltimore Ravens?

   a. The Ravens Dancers   b. Pop Bands   c. Baltimore Ravens Marching Band

79. Which Baltimore Raven was the unanimous NFL MVP pick?

   a. Joe Flacco   b. Lamar Jackson   c. Terrell Suggs

80. What was the name of the stadium, that, until 1998, the Baltimore Ravens had to share their home playing space with?

   a. Orioles Field   b. Maryland Park   c. Camden Yards

Answers: 71-b, 72-c, 73-b, 74-a, 75-c, 76-a, 77-b, 78-c, 79-b, 80-a

81. Who are the Cleveland Browns named for?

    a. their first head coach   b. the brown in their uniforms c. Brownie the Mascot

82. Which division do the Cleveland Browns play in?

    a. AFC North   b. AFC Central   c. AFC East

83. Between 2002 and 2020, what percentage of all of the Cleveland Browns games have the won?

    a. 1/3   b. ½   c. 2/3

84. What is the name of the Cleveland Browns home stadium?

    a. Ohio Field   b. Cleveland Stadium   c. FirstEnergy Stadium

85. Who is the Cleveland Browns biggest rival, known as the "Turnpike Rivalry"?

    a. Cincinnati Bengals   b. Detroit Lions   c. Pittsburgh Steelers

86. The Cleveland Browns had a famous fan in which 1950s rock n roller?

    a. Elvis   b. Jerry Lee Lewis   c. Chuck Berry

87. What is the name of the official Cleveland Browns fan club?

    a. Browns Fans   b. Browns Busters   c. Brown Backers

88. How many Cleveland Browns are in the Pro Football Hall of Fame?

    a. 26   b. 30   c. 34

89. Which former Cleveland Browns player went on to be their coach, as well as the head coach for one of their biggest rivals?

    a. Coach Cowher   b. Paul Brown   c. Sam Wyche

90. What is the Cleveland Browns' mascot name?

    a. Blackie the Bug   b. Brownie the Elf   c. Brownie the Gnome

Answers: 81-a, 82-b, 83-a, 84-c, 85-c, 86-a, 87-c, 88-a, 89-a, 90-b

91. What is the name of the Detroit Lions mascot?

    a. Lenny the Lion   b. Lorry the Lion   c. Rowry the Lion

92. What are the official colors of the Detroit Lions?

    a. blue and silver   b. blue and red   c. blue and white

93. What is the name of the Detroit Lions home Stadium?

    a. Lion's Den   b. Ford Field   c. Detroit Stadium

94. When was the Detroit Lions founded?

    a. 1920   b. 1930   c. 1940

95. What American holiday does the Detroit Lions play on annually?

    a. Halloween   b. Christmas   c. Thanksgiving

96. From 1934-1940, which college shared its football stadium with the Detroit Lions?

    a. Michigan State University b. University of Michigan c. University of Detroit

97. How many times have the Detroit Lions won the Super Bowl?

    a. 5   b. 3   c. 0

98. What did the Detroit Lions add in 2016 in the hopes to gain more fans?

    a. cheerleaders   b. marching bands   c. fireworks

99. The Detroit Lions biggest rivalry is called the Great Lakes Classic, with which other NFL team?

    a. Chicago Bears   b. Cleveland Browns   c. Pittsburgh Steelers

100. Who is the most recent Detroit Lion to enter the Pro Football Hall of Fame?

    a. Bill Dudley   b. Calvin Johnson   c. Alex Karras

Answers: 91-c, 92-a, 93-b, 94-b, 95-c, 96-c, 97-c, 98-a, 99-a, 100-b

101. When were the Cincinnati Bengals founded?

    a. 1947   b. 1957   c. 1967

102. Which division do the Cincinnati Bengals play in?

    a. AFC North b. NFC North   c. AFC Central

103. What are the Cincinnati Bengals official colors?

    a. black, white, red   b. black, white, blue c. black, white, orange

104. What is the name of the Cincinnati Bengals' home field?

    a. Paul Brown Stadium b. Bengals Field c. Ohio Field

105. How many Super Bowls have the Cincinnati Bengals won?

    a. 8   b. 4   c. 0

106. Which team were the Cincinnati Bengals uniforms based of off?

    a. New York Jets   b. Dallas Cowboys   c. Cleveland Browns

107. What is the name of the Bengals cheerleading squad?

    a. The Ben-Gals   b. The Cin-Girls c. The Begal Girls

108. In 2016, the Bengals introduced a new uniform called what?

    a. Bengal Blue b. Color Rush c. Orange Play

109. Which Bengals Pro Football Hall of Famer also served as a head coach?

    a. Anthony Munoz   b. Boomer Esiason   c. Vinny Testaverde

110. What kind of animal is the Cincinnati mascot?

    a. Tiger b. Lion c. Panther

Answers: 101-a, 102-a, 103-c, 104-a, 105-c, 106-c, 107-a, 108-b, 109-a, 110-a

111. When were the Carolina Panthers founded?

    a. 1990   b. 1993   c. 1995

112. What is the name of the Panthers home field?

    a. Bank of America Stadium   b. US Bank Field   c. Soldier Field

113. What are the Carolina Panthers official colors?

    a. blue, white, red   b. blue, white, black   c. blue, black, silver

114. How many Super Bowls have the Panthers won?

    a. 1   b. 2   c. 3

115. What is the Panthers' mascot name?

    a. Black Panther   b. Black Kat   c. Sir Purr

116. What conference is the Carolina Panthers in?

    a. NFC South   b. AFC South   c. NFC East

117. What is the name of the Carolina Panthers cheerleading squad?

    a. Panther Dancers   b. Carolina Tophats   c. Carolina Cheerers

118. What is the Carolina Panthers official halftime show drumline name?

    a. Carolina Drummers   b. Panther Pounders   c. Purr-Cussion

119. Which state do the Panthers represent?

    a. North Carolina   b. South Carolina   c. Both Carolinas

120. Who is the Panthers career passing leader?

    a. Cam Newton   b. John Kasay   c. Jonathan Stewart

Answers: 111-b, 112-a, 113-c, 114-b, 115-c, 116-a, 117-b, 118-c, 119-c, 120-a

121. In which conference does the Atlanta Falcons play?

    a. NFC South   b. AFC South   c. NFC Central

122. In what year was the Atlanta Falcons founded?

    a. 1945   b. 1955   c. 1965

123. What is the name of the Atlanta Falcons home field?

    a. Arrowhead Stadium   b. Mile High Stadium   c. Mercedes-Benz Stadium

124. What are the Atlanta Falcons official colors?

    a. black, white, red   b. black, white, blue   c. black, white, green

125. Who was the Atlanta Falcons' first head coach?

    a. Dan Reeves   b. Norb Turner   c. Wade Phillips

126. What year did the Atlanta Falcons have their first winning season?

    a. 1969   b. 1970   c. 1971

127. In which decade did the Atlanta Falcons not play a single playoff game?

    a. 1970s   b. 1980s   c. 1990s

128. Who was the Atlanta Falcons first round pick in 2001?

    a. Michael Strahan   b. Michael Shanahan   c. Michael Vick

129. What was the Atlanta Falcons Home Field until 1991?

    a. Atlanta-Fulton County Stadium   b. Falcon Field   c. Georgia Dome

130. Where did Atlanta Falcons quarterback Matt Ryan attend college?

    a. Bentley College   b. Brandeis University   c. Boston College

Answers: 121-a, 122-c, 123-c, 124-a, 125-a, 126-c, 127-b, 128-c, 129-a, 130-c

131. What was the Jacksonville Jaguars record in 2020?

    a. 15-1 b. 1-15 c. 8-8

132. What are the Jacksonville Jaguars official colors?

    a. teal, black, gold   b. teal, white, grey   c. teal, gold, purple

133.What is the name of the Jacksonville Jaguars home field?

    a. US Bank Arena   b. Bank of America Field   c. TIAA Field

134. What is the name of the Jacksonville Jaguar mascot?

    a. Jackie   b. Jaxson de Ville   c. Jag-Kitty

135. How many Super Bowls have the Jacksonville Jaguars won?

    a. 0   b. 1   c. 2

136. When were the Jacksonville Jaguars founded?

    a. 1983   b. 1993   c. 2003

137. What is the name of the Jacksonville Jaguars cheerleading squad?

    a. The Jag Girls b. The Jags   c. The Jacksonville Roar

138. Who was the Jacksonville Jaguars first head coach?

    a. Tony Dungy   b. Mike Tomlin c. Tom Coughlin

139. Which conference does the Jacksonville Jaguars play in?

    a. NFC South   b. AFC East   c. AFC South

140. Which college bowl game uses the Jacksonville Jaguars' stadium?

    a. Gator Bowl   b. Rose Bowl   c. Orange Bowl

Answers: 131-b, 132-a, 133-c, 134-b, 135-a, 136-b, 137-c, 138-c
         139-c, 140-a

141. When were the Tampa Bay Buccaneers found?

   a. 1974 b. 1984 c. 1994

142. What is the name of the Tampa Bay Buccaneers home field?

   a. Raymond James Stadium   b. Bucs Field   c. Tampa Stadium

143. What are the official colors of the Tampa Bay Buccaneers?

a. red, orange, blue, black   b, red, pink, pewter, black   c. red, orange, pewter, black

144. Who is the Tampa Bay Buccaneers mascot?

   a. Captain Bay   b. Captain Hook   c. Captain Fear

145. What division does the Tampa Bay Buccaneers play in?

   a. NFC South   b. NFC East   c. AFC South

146. How many Super Bowls has the Tampa Bay Buccaneers won?

   a. 2   b. 4   c. 6

147. How many Tampa Bay Buccaneers are in the Pro Football Hall of Fame?

   a. 5.   b. 7   c. 9

148. What did the Tampa Bay Buccaneers cheerleading squad change their name to, from the "Swash-Buc-Lers," in 1999?

   a. The Tampa Bay Cheerleaders   b. The Bay Girls   c. The Bay Dancers

149. What made for TV movie centers around a Tampa Bay Buccaneer and his friendship with a differently abled local child?

   a. Rudy   b. The Replacements   c. The Ricky Bell Story

150. What former pro wrestler and Governor of Minnesota did Tampa Bay Buccaneers radio play by play in 1990?

   a. Jesse Ventura   b. Hulk Hogan   c. John Cena

Answers: 141-a, 142-a, 143-c, 144-c, 145-a, 146-a, 147-b, 148-a, 149-c 150-a

151. What is the name of the Miami Dolphins home field?

a. Hard Rock Stadium   b. Miami Field   c. Florida Field

152. What conference do the Miami Dolphins play in?

a. AFC South   b. AFC East   c. NFC East

153. What is the name of the Miami Dolphins mascot?

a. Fishy   b. Rocky   c. T.D.

154. What are the Miami Dolphins official colors?

a. aqua, orange, white   b. aqua, orange, black   c. aqua, red, white

155. How many Super Bowls has the Miami Dolphins won?

a. 0   b. 1   c. 2

156. In what football season did the Miami Dolphins have an undefeated record?

a. 1971   b. 1972   c. 1973

157. The Miami Dolphins Cheerleaders were originally named after which team sponsor?

a. Starbrite Car Polish   b. Marlboro Cigarettes   c. Coca-Cola

158. In the 1970s, TV football commentators gave the Miami Dolphins defense what ironic nickname?

a. No Name Defense   b. Darn Good Defense   c. Doofy Defense

159. Who was the Miami Dolphins first head coach?

a. Jimmie Johnson   b. Don Shula   c. George Wilson

160. How any jersey numbers have the Miami Dolphins retired?

a. 3   b. 4   c. 5

Answers: 151-a, 152-b, 153-c, 154-a, 155-c, 156-b, 157-a, 158-a, 159-c, 160-a

161. Where is Tennessee is the Titans home field?

    a. Memphis   b. Nashville   c. Chattanooga

162. What is the name of the Tennessee Titans home field?

    a. Titan Stadium   b. Tennessee Field   c. Nissan Stadium

163. What are the Tennessee Titans official team colors?

    a. blue, red, silver, white   b. blue, red, black, white   c. blue, black, silver, white

164. In which conference does the Tennessee Titans play?

    a. AFC South   b. NFC South   c. AFC Central

165. How many Super Bowls have the Tennessee Titans won?

    a. 5   b. 3   c. 0

166. Who is the Tennessee Titans quarterback in 2020?

    a. Ryan Tannehill   b. Cam Newton c. Ben Roethlisberger

167. How many Tennessee Titans are in the Pro Football Hall of Fame?

    a. 4   b. 6   c. 8

168. What is the name of the Tennessee Titans mascot?

    a. The Titan   b. Zeus   c. T-Rac

169. The Tennessee Titans are an expansion team from the Houston Oilers, who were founded in what year?

    a. 1959 b. 1969 c. 1969

170. Who was the first head coach of the Tennessee Titans?

    a. Mike Munchak   b. Mike Vrabel c. Jeff Fischer

Answers: 161-b, 162-c, 163-a, 164-a, 165-c, 166-a, 167-c, 168-c, 169-a
170-c

171. How many Super Bowls have the Indianapolis Colts won?

    a. 0   b. 2   c. 4

172. What are the official colors of the Indianapolis Colts?

    a. white, blue, grey   b. white, blue, green   c. white, black, red

173. The Indianapolis Colts originally came from what east coast city?

    a. Washington, DC   b. New York City   c. Baltimore

174. In what year were the Indianapolis Colts founded in their original city?

    a. 1953   b. 1963   c. 1973

175. What is the name of the Indianapolis Colts home field?

    a. Colts Stadium   b. Indy 500 Field   c. Lucas Oil Stadium

176. What is the name of the Indianapolis Colts mascot?

    a. Colty   b. Blue   c. Gallop

177. Which conference does the Indianapolis Colts play for?

    a. NFC South   b. AFC South   c. AFC North

178. Who was the Indianapolis Colts first draft pick in 1998?

    a. Peyton Manning   b. Tom Brady   c. Deion Sanders

179. How many jersey numbers have the Indianapolis Colts retired?

    a. 12   b. 8   c. 4

180. How many players do the Indianapolis Colts have in the Pro Football Hall of Fame (including the Baltimore years)?

    a. 20   b. 18   c. 15

Answers: 171-b, 172-a, 173-c, 174-a, 175-c, 176-a, 177-b, 178-a, 179-b, 180-c

181. What are the official colors of the Houston Texans?

    a. red, white, blue   b. red, gold, blue   c. red, silver, blue

182. What conference does the Houston Texans play for?

    a. NFC South   b. AFC Central c. AFC South

183. What is the name of the Houston Texans mascot?

    a. Bullseye   b. Toro   c. Chuck

184. What is the Houston Texans fight song?

    a. Go Texans Go   b. Texans Fight   c. Football Time in Houston

185. What is the name of the Houston Texans home field?

    a. NRG Stadium   b. Houston Stadium   c. Texans Field

186. What was the name of the previous NFL team in Houston?

    a. Houston Rockets   b. Houston Heroes c. Houston Oilers

187. How many Super Bowls have the Houston Texans won?

    a. 5   b. 3   c. 0

188. What is the name for the rivalry game between the Houston Texans and the Dallas Cowboys?

    a. Governor's Cup   b. Battle for Texas   c. Interstate Rivalry

189. What is the name for the Houston Texans cheerleading squad?

    a. Houston Texans Cheerleading Squad b. Texans Cheer Team c. Houston Girls

190. What is the Houston Texans 45-member band called?

    a. Bull Pen Pep Band   b. Texans Pep Band   c. Pep Poppers

Answers: 181-a, 182-c, 183-b, 184-c, 185-a, 186-c, 187-c, 188-a, 189-a 190-a

191. What division does the Dallas Cowboys play in?

    a. NFC South   b. NFC North   c. NFC East

192. What are the official colors of the Dallas Cowboys?

    a. red, silver, white b. navy, silver, white c. navy, gold, white

193. What is the name of the Dallas Cowboys home field?

    a. Dallas Stadium   b. Arlington Field   c. AT&T Stadium

194. What is the name of the Dallas Cowboys mascot?

    a. Howdy   b. Rowdy   c. Bucky

195. How may Super Bowls have the Dallas Cowboys won?

    a. 3   b. 4   c. 5

196. In what year was the Dallas Cowboys founded?

    a. 1960   b. 1970   c. 1980

197. What is the Dallas Cowboys logo?

    a. blue five-pointed star   b. a cowboy hat   c. the Texas flag

198. What sound is played after every Dallas Cowboys score at their home games?

    a. a train horn   b. a horse whinny   c. a bull stampede

199. Who was the Dallas Cowboys first head coach?

    a. Tom Landry b. Jimmie Johnson   c. Bill Parcells

200. The Dallas Cowboys do not retire jersey numbers, but how many jerseys are officially 'inactive?'

    a. 2   b. 4   c. 6

Answers: 191-a, 192-b, 193-c, 194-b, 195-c, 196-a, 197-a, 198-a, 199-a 200-b

201. Which division do the Denver Broncos play for?

    a. NFC South   b. AFC East   c. AFC West

202. What is the name of the Denver Broncos home field?

    a. Empower Field at Mile High   b. Denver Field   c. Bronco Field

203. What are the official colors of the Denver Broncos?

    a. orange, black, blue   b. orange, navy, white   c. orange, red, white

204. What year were the Denver Broncos established?

    a. 1960   b. 1970   c. 1980

205. How many Super Bowl championships have the Denver Broncos won?

    a. 1   b. 3   c. 5

206. What is the name of the mascot of the Denver Broncos?

    a. Thunder   b. Bucky   c. Brownie

207. Who was the Denver Broncos MVP of Super Bowl XXXIII?

    a. Von Miller   b. John Elway   c. Terrell Davis

208. How many Denver Broncos are in the Pro Football Hall of Fame?

    a. 2   b. 5   c. 8

209. As of 2020, who is the Denver Broncos quarterback?

    a. Jeff Driskel   b. Peyton Manning   c. John Elway

210. As of 2020, who is the Denver Broncos head coach?

    a. Vic Fangio   b. Bill Parcells   c. Rob Ryan

Answers: 201-c, 202-a, 203-b, 204-a, 205-c, 206-a, 207-b, 208-b, 209-a
210-a

221. What is the name of the Los Angeles Chargers home field?

   a. L.A. Stadium b. Chargers Field   c. SoFi Stadium

222. The Los Angeles Chargers home field is actually in which California city?

   a. Sacramento b. San Diego   c. Inglewood

223. What are the official colors of the Los Angeles Chargers?

   a. blue, gold, white   b. blue, red, white   c. blue, orange, white

224. In what division do the Los Angeles Chargers play?

   a. AFC West   b. AFC South   c. AFC Central

225. Which city did the Los Angeles Chargers relocate from in 2019?

   a. San Francisco   b. San Diego   c. St. Louis

226. What was the Los Angeles Chargers prior theme song before moving to Los Angeles?

   a. Go Chargers Go!   b. Score Score Score! c. Super Chargers

227. What is the name of the Los Angeles Chargers Cheerleaders?

   a. Charger Girls   b. Charger Cheerleaders   c. Charger Dancers

228. Which Watt brother plays for the Los Angeles Chargers?

   a. TJ   b. Derek   c. JJ

229. Who is the 2021 Los Angeles Chargers head coach?

   a. Brandon Staley   b. Arthur Smith c. Robert Saleh

230. When was the original Los Angeles Chargers founded?

   a. 1939 b. 1949 c. 1959

Answers: 221-c, 222-c, 223-a, 224-a, 225-b, 226-c, 227-a, 228-b, 229-a 230-c

231. When did the Las Vegas Raiders leave Oakland, CA?

    a. 2020   b. 2010   c. 2000

232. What are the Las Vegas Raiders official colors?

    a. black and gold   b. black and silver   c. blue and blue

233. What is the Las Vegas Raiders mascot's name?

    a. Raider Ron   b. Raider Dave   c. Raider Rusher

234. What is the Las Vegas Raiders fight song?

    a. Go Raiders Go   b. Autumn Wind   c. Winter Football

235. What division do the Las Vegas Raiders play in?

    a. AFC South   b. AFC West   c. NFC West

236. What is the name of the Las Vegas Raiders home field?

    a. Allegiant Stadium   b. Raiders Field   c. Nevada Stadium

237. What is the name of the Las Vegas Raiders cheerleading squad?

    a. The Raiderettes   b. The Dancing Raiders   c. The Raider Girls

238. How many Super Bowl Championships have the Las Vegas Raiders won?

    a. 0   b. 2   c. 3

239. Who was the Las Vegas Raiders first head coach?

    a. Eddie Erdelatz   b. Vince Lombardi   c. Bill Madden

240. Who is the 2021 Las Vegas Raiders quarterback?

    a. Cam Newton b. Derek Carr   c. Ben Roethlisberger

Answers: 231-a, 232-b, 233-c, 234-b, 235-b, 236-a, 237-a, 238-0, 239-a
240-b

241. What division do the Kansas City Chiefs play for?

    a. AFC West   b. NFC West   c. AFC Central

242. What are the official colors of the Kansas City Chiefs?

    a. red, blue, gold b. red, gold, white c. red, silver, white

243. What is the name of the Kansas City Chiefs home field?

    a. Missouri Stadium   b. Arrowhead Stadium   c. MetLife Stadium

244. What is the name of the Kansas City Chiefs mascot?

    a. KC Wolf   b. Arrow   c. Chief

245. How many times have the Kansas City Chiefs won the Super Bowl?

    a. 2   b. 4   c. 6

246. What is the Kansas City Chiefs cheerleader squad called?

    a. ChiefLeaders   b. ChiefsCheer   c. Chiefs Cheerleaders

247. Who is the Kansas City Chiefs current quarterback in 2021?

    a. Tom Brady   b. Ryan Tanehill   c. Patrick Mahomes

248. How many jersey numbers have the Kansas City Chiefs retired?

    a. 8   b. 10   c. 12

249. How many Kansas City Chiefs are enshrined in the Pro Football Hall of Fame?

    a. 11   b. 12   c. 14

250. What is the name of the pep band that played at half time at the Kansas City Chiefs home games?

    a. The Zing Band   b. The Chiefs Band c. The Halftime Hitmakers

Answers: 241-a, 242-b, 243-b, 244-a, 245-a, 246-c, 247-c, 248-8, 249-c 250-a

251. What division do the Minnesota Vikings play for?

    a. AFC North   **b. NFC North**   c. NFC Central

252. How many times have the Minnesota Vikings won the Super Bowl?

    a. 4   b. 2   c. 0

253. What are the official colors of the Minnesota Vikings?

    a. purple, gold, white   b. purple, silver, white   c. blue, white, black

254. What is the Minnesota Vikings mascot's name?

    a. Viktor the Viking   b. Val the Viking   c. Vinny the Viking

255. What is the Minnesota Vikings fight song?

    a. Score Vikings   b. Skol, Vikings   c. Go Vikings Go

256. Who has the biggest rivalry with the Minnesota Vikings?

    a. Dallas Cowboys   b. Kansas City Chiefs   c. Green Bay Packers

257. What is the name of the Minnesota Vikings horn?

    a. Gjallarhorn   b. Mollarhorn   c. VikingHorn

258. What is the name of the purple hats with blond braids worn by Minnesota Vikings fans?

    a. Hagar Hats   b. Honor Hats   c. Helga Hats

259. What is the name of Minnesota Vikings home field?

    a. US Bank Stadium   b. Vikings Field   c. Soldier Field

260. In what year were the Minnesota Vikings founded?

    a.1940   b. 1950   c. 1960

Answers: 251-b, 252-c, 253-a, 254-a, 255-b, 256-c, 257-a, 258-a, 259-a, 260-c

261. In what year were the Chicago Bears founded?

    a. 1920   b. 1930   c. 1940

262. What were the Chicago Bears called for their first season?

    a. Chicago Illini   b. Chicago Staleys   c. Chicago Cats

263. What is the Chicago Bears fight song?

    a. Bear Down   b. Score, GO, Bears   c. Go Bears Go

264. What are the official colors of the Chicago Bears?

    a. black, orange, white   b. red, yellow, white   c. navy, orange, white

265. What division do the Chicago Bears play in?

    a. NFC North   b. NFC Central   c. AFL North

266. What is the name of the Chicago Bears mascot?

    a. Staley da Bear   b. Billy da Bear   c. Bobby the Bear

267. How many Super Bowls have the Chicago Bears won?

    a. 5   b. 3   c. 1

268. What philanthropy is the Chicago Bears affiliated with?

    a. Food Banks of Chicago   b. Homelessness of Chicago   c. A Safe Place

269. The Chicago Bears had a cheerleading squad until 1985, what were they called?

    a. The Chicago Honey Bears   b. The Chicago Cheerleaders   c. The Chicago Dancers

270. Which former Chicago Bears coach appears as himself in several comedy movies?

    a. Mike Nagy   b. Mike Ditka   c. John Fox

Answers: 261-a, 262-b, 263-a, 264-c, 265-a, 266-a, 267-c, 268-c, 269-a 270-b

271. How many Super Bowls have the New Orleans Saints won?

    a. 2   b. 1   c. 0

272. What division do the New Orleans Saints play in?

    a. AFC South   b. NFC South   c. NFC Central

273. What is the name of the New Orleans Saints logo?

    a. Watermark   b. Hashtag   c. Fleur-de-Lis

274. What are the official colors of the New Orleans Saints?

    a. black and gold   b. black and silver   c. black and red

275. What is the name of the New Orleans Saints home field?

    a. Saints Stadium   b. New Orleans Field   c. Mercedes-Benz Superdome

276. What is the name of the New Orleans Saints fight song?

    a. Go Win Saints!   b. TD Saints   c. When the Saints Go Marching In

277. What is the name of the New Orleans Saints mascot?

    a. Sir Saint   b. Saint Orleans   c. Saint TD

278. What is the name of the New Orleans Saints cheerleading squad?

    a. The Saintsations   b. The Saint Dancers   c. New Orleans Dancers

279. As of 2021, who is the quarterback of the New Orleans Saints?

    a. Eli Manning   b. Patrick Mahomes   c. Drew Brees

280. Who is the 2021 head coach of the New Orleans Saints?

    a. Doug Pederson   b. Sam Payton   c. Andy Reid

Answers: 271-b, 272-b, 273-c, 274-a, 275-c, 276-c, 277-a, 278-a, 279-c, 280-b

281. How many Super Bowl Championships have the San Francisco 49ers won?

    a. 3   b. 5   c.7

282. What are the official colors of the San Francisco 49ers?

    a. red and black b. blue and black   c. red and gold

283. What division do the San Francisco 49ers play for?

    a. NFC West   b. AFC West   c. NFC North

284. What is the name of the San Francisco 49ers' mascot?

    a. Sourdough Sam   b. San Man   c. Franny

285. What is the name of the San Francisco 49ers home field?

    a. Niners Field   b. Levi's Stadium   c. San Fran Field

286. What is the significance of the number '49' to the team?

    a. 1849 gold rush in CA b. 49 players on the roster c. It was random

287. What number does the San Francisco 49ers mascot wear?

    a. 00   b. 49   c. 99

288. Which San Francisco 49ers quarterback started the National Anthem protest?

    a. Colin Kaepernick   b. Steve Young   c. Jimmy Garopollo

289. How many jersey numbers have the San Francisco 49ers retired?

    a. 10 b. 12 c. 14

290. Who is the 2021 head coach of the San Francisco 49ers?

    a. Bill Belichick   b. Andy Reid c. Kyle Shanahan

Answers: 281-b, 282-c, 283-a, 284-a, 285-b, 286-a, 287-b, 288-a, 289-b, 290-c

291. What division do the Arizona Cardinals play in?

    a. NFC Central   b. NFC West   c. AFC East

292. What are the official Arizona Cardinals colors?

    a. red, white, blue   b. red, white, black c. red, yellow, white

293. When were the Arizona Cardinals founded?

    a. 1984   b. 1994   c. 2004

294. What is the name of the Arizona Cardinals mascot?

    a. Big Red   b. Red Tide c. Cardy

295. What is the name of the Arizona Cardinals home field?

    a. State Farm Stadium   b. Arizona Field   c. Cards Field

296. How many Super Bowls have the Arizona Cardinals won?

    a. 2 b. 1 c. 0

297. Who is the 2021 Arizona Cardinals quarterback?

    a. Kyle Murray   b. Kyle Shanahan   c. Keith Murray

298. Which Watt brother plays for the Arizona Cardinals?

    a. Derek   b. TJ   c. JJ

299. How many jersey numbers have the Arizona Cardinals retired?

    a. 7 b. 5 c. 3

300. How has been the Arizona Cardinals head coach since 2019?

    a. Kliff Kingbury   b. Mike Shanahan c. Mike Tomlin

Answers: 291-b, 292-b, 293-b, 294-a, 295-a, 296-c, 297-a, 298-c, 299-a, 300-a

301. When was the (current) Los Angeles Rams founded?

    a. 2000   b. 2008   c. 2016

302. What division do the Los Angeles Rams play for?

    a. NFC West   b. AFC West   c. NFC South

303. What are the official colors of the Los Angeles Rams?

    a. blue and grey   b. blue and gold   c. blue and white

304. What is the name of the mascot for the Los Angeles Rams?

    a. Rampage   b. Rammer   c. Rambo

305. What is the name of the Los Angeles Rams home field?

    a. Rams Field   b. SoFi Stadium   c. Levi Stadium

306. What city did the Rams NOT play in before coming to Los Angeles?

    a. Reno   b. St. Louis   c. Cleveland

307. The Rams were the first team to have what element on their helmets?

    a. interior padding   b. logo   c. a cage

308. Who is the current quarterback, as of 2021?

    a. Jared Goff   b. Terry Bradshaw   c. Ed Hodges

309. What city do the Los Angeles Rams actually play in?

    a. San Diego   b. Sacramento   c. Inglewood

310. How many Super Bowls did this incarnation of the Los Angeles Rams win?

    a. 5   b. 3   c. 0

Answers: 301-c, 302-a, 303-b, 304-a, 305-b, 306-a, 307-b, 308-a, 309-c 310-c

311. In what year were the Green Bay Packers founded?

    a. 1919   b. 1929   c. 1939

312. Who owns the Green Bay Packers?

    a. Robert Kraft   b. Green Bay Packers, Inc.   c. Art Rooney

313. What are the official NFL colors of the Green Bay Packers?

    a. green and white   b. green and gold   c. green and grey

314. What division do the Green Bay Packers play for?

    a. NFC North   b. NFC Central c. AFC North

315. What is the Green Bay Packers fight song?

    a. Go Green Go b. TD Packers!   c. Go You Packers Go

316. What is the name of the Green Bay Packers home field?

    a. Packers Stadium   b. Green Bay Field c. Lambeau Field

317. How long did famous quarterback Brett Favre play for the Green Bay Packers?

    a. 14 years   b. 22 years c. 25 years

318. How many Super Bowls have the Green Bay Packers won?

    a. 4   b. 6   c. 8

319. In 1919, when shares of Green Bay Packers were sold to the people of Green Bay, what did a share cost?

    a. $10   b. $5   c. $1

320. What is the nickname of the Green Bay Packers fanbase?

    a. Cheeseheads   b. Bayfans   c. Greenies

Answers: 311-a, 312-b, 313-b, 314-a, 315-c, 316-c, 317-c, 318-a, 319-b, 320-a

DID YOU KNOW?

1. Because the NFL is considered a non-profit organization, it does not pay taxes.
2. IN 1967, the average Superbowl ticket price was $12.
3. The NFL is not the only professional football league currently operating in the USA; the biggest leagues other than the NFL are the Arena and XFL leagues which both play indoors, and the Gridiron Rival Professional League which plays outdoors.
4. Some NFL teams share stadiums with MLB teams, and when football and baseball seasons overlap, the baseball teams have priority. When the New York Mets played in the World Series in 1987, the New York Jets had to play their first *six* games on the road.
5. NFL games have been postponed or cancelled due to natural disasters such as earthquakes and hurricanes.
6. DeAngelo Williams, a running back with the Pittsburgh Steelers, lost his mother to breast cancer when she was 53 years old. Each year he pays for 53 women to receive mammograms in her honor.
7. In 2008, New York Giant Plaxico Burress accidentally shot himself in the eg in a crowded New York City nightclub.
8. The first televised NFL game was only viewed through 500 television sets.
9. The NFL season is the shortest sports season of any professional sports season in America.
10.   Fewer people get married on Super Bowl Sunday in the United States than on any other Sunday.

"Ability is what you're capable of doing. Motivation determines what you do. Attitude determines how well you do it." – Lou Holtz

If you enjoy this book, we have a very modest request: ***please take a few seconds to leave us a review on this book's Amazon product page.***

You can't imagine how pleased we are for the support, and we are doing our *best* to deliver you the best books.   We wish you only the best

Sincerely,

Brainy Tiger Team

IX. Other Important NFL Staff: Coaches, Managers, Owners

1. NFL Coach Bud Grant was a player before he was a coach, and was a professional player in another league as well. Which was one it?
    a. Basketball   b. Baseball   c. Hockey

2. Who was the head coach of the New York Jets during their winning 2008 season?
    a. Eric Mangini   b. Bill Belichick   c. Dan Shula

3. Which NFL Coach took the Patriots to a perfect 16-0 regular season record?
    a. Bill Belichick   b. Bill Parcells   c. Knute Rockne

4. Who was the first coach to win more than one Super Bowl?
    a. Tony Dungy   b. Mike Shanahan   c. Don Shula

5. Which coach won Super Bowls I and II?
    a. George Halas   b. Tom Brown   c. Vince Lombardi

6. How many female team owners are there in the NFL?
    a. 5 b. 7 c. 9

7. Which of the following cannot own an NFL team?
    a. married couples   b. family estates   c. religious organizations

8. Who was the first head coach who took a team to 6 Super Bowl appearances?
    a. Tom Landry   b. Vince Lombardi   c. Don Shula

9. Who was the Green Bay Packers first head coach?
    a. Vince Lombardi   b. Curly Lambeau   c. Red Grange

10. Which Steelers head coach won four Super Bowls in the 1970s?
    a. Tony Dungy   b. Chuck Noll   c. Mike Tomlin

Answers: 1-a, 2-a, 3-a, 4-c, 5-c, 6-c, 7-c, 8-c, 9-b, 10-b

11. Which head coach took the New York Jets to their only Super Bowl Victory?

    a. Weeb Ewbank   b. George Halas   c. Don Shula

12. As of the 2019 season, what percentage of NFL coaches have won 50 or more regular season games?

    a. 10% b. 20% c. 30%

13. Which NFL head coach never had a losing season?

    a. Chuck Noll   b. Bud Grant   c. John Madden

14. Which retired NFL coach's son Klint is the offensive coordinator for the Minnesota Vikings?

    a. Mike Tomlin   b. Mike Shanahan   c. Gary Kubiak

15. Which NFL coach has the most wins without winning a Super Bowl?

    a. Marty Schottenheimer   b. Buddy Parker   c. Marv Levy

16. What unusual building does Vince Lombardi, first coach of the New York Giants, have named after him?

    a. a library   b. a locker room   c. a service station

17. Who is the youngest head coach to win a Super Bowl?

    a. Jon Grudden   b. Mike Tomlin   c. Andy Reid

18. Which NFL head coach started "A Better LA," a charity aimed at Stopping gang activity in Los Angeles?

    a. Ron Rivera   b. Art Shell   c. Pete Carroll

19. What is the name of the ranch founded by NFL coach Bart Starr for troubled youth in his home state of Wisconsin?

    a. Wisconsin Boys Farm   b. Rawhide Boys Ranch   c. Runners Ranch

20. Which NFL head coach defeated his twin brother in Super Bowl 7?

    a. Bill Cower   b. Tony Dungy   c. John Harbough

Answers: 11-a, 12-b, 13-c, 14-c, 15-a, 16-c, 17-b, 18-c, 19-b, 20-c

21. Before an official "President" was chosen, who was the first 'temporary secretary' of the APFA (precursor to NFL)?
    b.   Joseph Carr   b. George Halas   c. Ralph Hay
22. In what year did the APFA's President standardize player contracts?
    a.   1920   b. 1922   c. 1924
23. In 1939, who was named the APFA's new President?
    a.   George Halas   b. Carl Storck   c. Vince Lombardi
24. In what year did the head of the league's title change to Commissioner?
    a.   1935   b. 1937   c. 1941
25. When Steelers co-owner Bert Bell was elected Commissioner in 1945, what was his annual salary?
    a. $15,000   b. $20,000   c. $25,000
26. Who is the current NFL Commissioner, as of 2021?
    a.   Paul Tagliabue   b. Roger Goodell   c. Pete Rozelle
27. What is the current NFL Commissioner's salary with bonuses?
    a. $24M   b. $34M   c. $44M
28. Which New York City family has been at least a partial owner of the New York Giants from its beginning?
    a.   The Smiths   b. The Guilianis   c. The Maras
29. How many non-American owners or partial owners of NFL are there (as of 2021)?
    a.   5   b. 4   c. 3
30. Which NFL team has the newest owner?
    a.   Tennessee Titans   b. Seattle Seahawks   c. New Orleans Saints

Answers: 21-a, 22-b, 23-b, 24-c, 25-b, 26-b, 27-c, 28-c, 29-c, 30-b

DID YOU KNOW?

1. The Houston Texans is the newest addition to the NFL.

2. The Dallas Cowboys is worth over 1.5 billion dollars.

3. In 1938, the Chicago Bears played in six games that ended in a tie.

4. Only 0.0008% of all high school football players will be drafted to the NFL.

5. The youngest NFL player was Amobi Okoye. He graduated from high school at 16, played college football and graduated at 19, and was drafted by the Houston Texans…as a teenager.

6. As of 2018, Brett Favre and Peyton Manning are the only two quarterbacks in history to have beaten all 32 NFL teams.

7. In 1993, the NFL moved the Superbowl out of Arizona because residents voted against recognizing Martin Luther King, Jr. Day.

8. The hottest and coldest NFL games on record were 109 and -13F…and the Dallas Cowboys played in both of them.

9. Terry Crewes, who played for the Los Angeles Rams in 1991 and would paint his teammates portraits.

10. Over 95% of NFL players' brains show signs of CTE (Chronic Traumatic Encephalopathy) on post-mortem examinations.

"Set your goals high, and don't stop till you get there." –
Bo Jackson

X. NFL Stadiums

1. Which NFL stadium was first to have a holding cell?

    a. New York Giants b. Philadelphia Eagles c. Jacksonville Jaguars

2. In which state do the New York Giants play their home games?

    a. Connecticut b. New Jersey c. Pennsylvania

3. What is the first stadium to use artificial grass (Astroturf)?

    a. The Astrodome (Houston) b. Lambeau Field (Green Bay)

    b. c. Soldier Field (Chicago)

4. This stadium is known as the "Toughest Place to Play," and the "Red Sea," because of the very loud fans. What is it called?

    a. Arrowhead Stadium b. Soldier Field c. MetLife Stadium

5. In which state is FedEx Field, home of The Washington Football Team (formerly the Washington Redskins)?

    a. Maryland b. Virginia c. Delaware

6. How many NFL stadiums have roofs (fixed or retractable)?

    a. 5 b. 7 c. 10

7. Which NFL stadium has the largest seating capacity?

    a. Candlestick Park b. The Superdome c. MetLife Stadium

8. Which city has hosted the most Super Bowls?

    a. Hard Rock Stadium, Miami b. Mercedes-Benz Stadium, Atlanta
    c. US Bank Stadium, Minneapolis

9. Which NFL stadium has a full-sized pirate ship in one end zone?

    a. State Farm b. Ray Jay c. Heinz Field

10. Which NFL team opted for renovation over a brand-new stadium, out of nostalgia and respect for its history?

    a. Chicago Bears b. Cleveland Browns c. Buffalo Bills

Answers: 1-b, 2-b, 3-a, 4-a, 5-a, 6-c, 7-c, 8-a, 9-b, 10-a

11. Which stadium has an HD video screen known as the "Jerry-Tron"?

    a. AT&T Stadium (Cowboys)   b. Lucas Oil Stadium Colts)

    c. Empower Field (Broncos)

12. Which stadium has a 12 story lighthouse?

    a. Gillette Stadium (Patriots) b. MetLife Stadium (Jets)

    c. Soldier Field (Bears)

13. Which team refers to a section of their stadium as The Dawg (Dog) Pound?

    a. Cleveland Browns b. L.A. Chargers c. Denver Broncos

14. What is the newest stadium in the NFL?

    a. Allegiant Stadium   b. Ford Field   c. Arrowhead Stadium

15. Which team's former stadium was know as the "Mistake by the Lake?"

    a. Cleveland Browns b. Pittsburgh Steelers c. Detroit Lions

16. Which NFL stadium was home to the Music City Miracle?

    a. Nissan Stadium   b. MetLife Stadium   c. Lambeau Field

17. Which stadium is the only one left in the NFL that is shared between two NFL teams?

    a. Mile High Stadium   b. MetLife Stadium   c. NRG Stadium

18. The Mercedes-Benz Superdome has the last remaining one of what in the NFL?

    a. Astroturf field   b. plastic seats c. fixed dome

19. Which NFL stadium appeared in an Emmy nominated movie?

    a. Arrowhead Stadium b. Lucas Oil Field c. Heinz Field

20. Which NFL stadium is also known as a football amusement park?

    a. AT&T Stadium b. US Bank Stadium c. Allegiant Stadium

Answers: 11-a, 12-a, 13-a, 14-a, 15-a, 16-a, 17-b, 18-c, 19-c, 20-a

21. Which stadium has a six-foot-tall drum that is struck four times, once for each quarter, before every game?

    a. Bank of America Stadium b. Levi's Stadium c. SoFi Stadium

22. Which stadium has a "Krewe of Honor" mural, honoring its first three greatest players in team history?

    a. MetLife Stadium b. Raymond James Stadium c. SoFi Stadium

23. Which NFL stadium has two 35-foot exact replica bottles of ketchup?

    a. Lambeau Field   b. Soldier Field   c. Heinz Stadium

24. Which NFL stadium has a glass wall that retracts, is seven stories tall, and is surrounded by over 100 restaurants?

    a. SoFi Stadium   b. Levi's Stadium   c. Lucas Oil Stadium

25. Which NFL Stadium has sustained earthquakes in 2014, 2015, 2019?

    a. Lumen Stadium   b. Allegiant Stadium   c. Levi's Stadium

26. Which NFL stadium has a life size ship outside to welcome fans?

    a. TIAA Bank Field   b. US Bank Stadium   c. Soldier Field

27. Whose stadium is nicknamed "The Linc?"

    a. Pittsburgh Steelers   b. Buffalo Bills c. Philadelphia Eagles

28. Which team has a horse gallop around their stadium at the opening of every game?

    a. Denver Broncos   b. Indianapolis Colts   c. Chicago Bears

29. Which NFL stadium is the least expensive to attend?

    a. Heinz Field   b. First Energy Stadium   c. Lambeau Field

30. At which NFL stadium will you experience 'table jumping at tailgating?'

    a. Bills Stadium   b. MetLife Stadium   c. Gillette Stadium

Answers: 21-a, 22-b, 23-c, 24-a, 25-a, 26-b, 27-c, 28-a, 29-b, 30-a

DID YOU KNOW?

1. Former NFL coach and commentator John Madden was so fearful of flying he only travelled on a coach bus.

2. Former NFL referee Ed Hochuli was the longest running referee—and was a lawyer, who officiated for the NFL as a side job.

3. In 2010, Brett Favre became the only active player in the NFL who was also a grandfather.

4. Over half of retired NFL players admit to taking prescription painkillers while playing for the NFL—most were taking them during a game.

5. Alex Smith, an NFL quarterback, took so many advanced courses in high school that he started college as a junior; he graduated two years early and was the first overall pick in the 2005 draft.

6. Quarterback Russell Wilson can trace his family tree back to the first century, where his earliest known relative was the St. Arnulf, Patron Saint of Beer.

7. John Madden now refers to the licensing of a video game in his name "The dumbest thing I did in my life."

8. NFL legend Walter Payton was an accomplished drummer in high school, and only agreed to join the football team when he was promised he wouldn't have to quit the marching band.

9. Actor and wrestler Dwayne "The Rock" Johnson tried and failed to make the NFL at age 24.

10. In 2009, the highest paid center in the NFL was Jason Brown—who quit football to become a farmer and donate his crops to food pantries.

"For every pass I caught in a game, I caught a thousand in practice." –Don Hutson

XI. Football Sayings and Player & Team Nicknames

1. Whose fans are told to "Defend the Den"?

    a. Chicago Bears b. Carolina Panthers c. Detroit Lions

2. Whose battle cry is "Here We Go!"

    a. Pittsburgh Steelers b. Arizona Cardinals c. New Orleans Saints

3. Which NFL team recorded a song and filmed an MTV video in the mid-80s in preparation for a Superbowl trip?

    a. The Chicago Bears "Shuffling Crew" b. NY Jets "Go Fly" c. Denver "Bucking Broncos"

4. Who was known as "The Bus"?

    a. Brett Favre   b. Jerome Bettis c. Michael Vick

5. Which NFL team has a mascot named "Who Dey?"

    a. Chicago Bears b. Baltimore Ravens c. Cincinnati Bengals

6. Which NFL team is also known as "America's Team?"

    a. New York Jets b. Dallas Cowboys c. New York Giants

7. Which NFL team's fans spell the team name as a chant?

    a. Jacksonville Jaguars b. Minnesota Vikings c. New York Jets

8. Whose slogan is "Fire the Cannons!"?

    a. Pittsburgh Steelers b. Tennessee Titans c. Tampa Bay Buccaneers

9. Which NFL player, and later Monday Night Football co-host, has the nickname "Broadway Joe?"

    a. Joe Montana   b. Joe Namath c.   Joe Smith

10. What is the motto of the Jacksonville Jaguars?

    a. Stand United   b. Mad Jags   c. Go Jags Go

Answers: 1-c, 2-a, 3-a, 4-b, 5-c, 6-b, 7-c, 8-c, 9-b, 10-a

11. Who was known as the Amish Rifle, because of his big beard?

    a. Ben Roethlisberger   b. Ryan Fitzpatrick   c. Ryan Tanehill

12. Whose nick name is the Blonde Bomber?

    a. Drew Brees   b. Joe Namath c. Terry Bradshaw

13. Who was known as Megatron?

    a. Calvon Johnson b. Wayne Johnson   c. Lawrence Taylor

14. What was Jerry Rice's nickname, given in college because there was no catch in the world he couldn't touch?

    a. Grabber   b. Master   c. World

15. This nickname came from the Red Grange's off-season job, what is it?

    a. Wheaton Ice Man   b. Wheaton Salesman c. Wheaton Sitter

16. Which coach received his nickname "Big Tuna" because he resembled advertising cartoon "Charlie the Tuna?"

    a. Bill Parcells   b. Bill Belachick c. Jim Harbaugh

17. Who was known as "The Sherriff?"

    a. Eli Manning   b. Peyton Manning   c. Tom Brady

18. Who was known as 'Sweetness' for his sweet moves on the field?

    a. Peyton Manning   b. Walter Payton   c. Deion Sanders

19. Whose nickname was The Playmaker, due to his ability to create scoring opportunities?

    a. Michael Irvin   b. Michael Oher   c. Michael Vick

20. Who is the Comeback Kid?

    a. Joe Montana   b. Tom Brady c. Eli Manning

Answers: 11-b, 12-c, 13-a, 14-c, 15-a, 16-a, 17-b, 18-b, 19-a, 20-a

21. What was the nickname of Atlanta Falcons linebacker Jessie Tuggle?

    a. The Hammer   b. The Saw   c. The Knife

22. Whose fans cheered for the 'Monsters of the Midway?'

    a. Minnesota Vikings   b. Kansas City Chiefs   c. Chicago Bears

23. Which team is known as The Blue Wave?

    a. New York Giants   b. Seattle Seahawks   c. Denver Broncos

24. Whose defensive line was known as the Purple People Eaters?

    a. Minnesota Vikings   b. New England Patriots c. Buffalo Bills

25. Whose wide receiver corps was known as the Legion of Vroom?

    a. Cleveland Browns   b. Las Vegas Raiders   c. Dallas Cowboys

26. Whose 1970s defense was known as the Orange Crush?

    a. Miami Dolphins   b. Chicago Bears   c. Denver Broncos

27. Who is the Alabama Antelope?

    a. Ed Reed   b. Red Grange c. Don Hutson

28. Who is Deebo?

    a. JJ Watt   b. Antonio Brown   c. James Harrison

29. Who is Gronk?

    a. Rob Gronkowski   b. Brett Favre   c. Ben Roethlisberger

30. What was Roger Staubach's nickname?

    a. Lightening Kid   b. Thunder Kid   c. Comeback Kid

Answers: 21-a, 22-c, 23-b, 24-a, 25-a, 26-c, 27-c, 28-c, 29-a, 30-c

31. Which team is known as the Evil Empire?

    a. New Orleans Saints   b. New England Patriots   c. New York Giants

32. Who was the Iron Curtain?

    a. Buffalo Bills defense   b. Pittsburgh Steelers defense c. New York Jets

33. Who are the G-Men?

    a. New York Giants   b. New York Jets   c. Carolina Panthers

34. Who is Mr Big Chest?

    a. Russell Wilson   b. Tom Brady   c. Antonio Brown

35. Who is The Freak?

    a. Troy Polamalu b. Randy Moss c. Brett Favre

36. Who is The Fridge?

    a. Walter Perry b. Zach Banner c. Trent Brown

37. Whose nickname is The Walrus?

    a. Andy Reed   b. Gene Upshaw   c. Red Grange

38. Which NFL stadium is known as The Big Crabcake?

    a. MetLife Stadium   b. Arrowhead Stadium c. M&T Bank Stadium

39. What is the nickname for the seating section under the scoreboard at Bills Stadium?

    a. The Rockpile b. The Bleachers   c. The Cheap Seats

40. Which NFL team's stadium's nickname is called The Frozen Tundra?

    a. Allegiant Stadium   b. Lambeau Field   c. FirstEnergy Stadium

Answers: 31-b, 32-b, 33-a, 34-c, 35-b, 36-a, 37-a, 38-c, 39-a, 40-b

41. Which NFL stadium is known as The Razor?

    a. Gillette Stadium   b. Raymond James Stadium   c. Bills Stadium

42. What is the nickname of Bank of America Stadium?

    a. The Safe   b. The Locker   c. The Vault

43. What is the nickname of Buffalo Bills Stadium?

    a. The Ralph   b. The Ray   c. The Rob

44. Whose fans are known as the Sea of Red?

    a. San Francisco 49ers   b. Kansas City Chiefs   c. Detroit Lions

45. Which teams' fans are known as 'Boo Birds,' who will shout BOO even at their own team?

    a. Arizona Cardinals   b. Atlanta Falcons   c. Philadelphia Eagles

46. What is the name for the New Orleans Saints fans who throw massive pre game parties?

    a. Saints Sinners   b. NOLA Fans   c. Big Easy Mafia

47. Which NFL teams' fans are called Flameheads, because of the flame-like hats they wear to games?

    a. Las Vegas Raiders   b. Houston Texans   c. Tennessee Titans

48. Whose fans are known as 'Who Dat Nation?'

    a. New Orleans Saints   b. Minnesota Vikings   c. Seattle Seahawks

49. Whose fans are the '4th Phase?'

    a. Chicago Bears   b. Washington Football Team   c. Baltimore Ravens

50. Whose fans are the 'Mob Squad?'

    a. New York Giants   b. Los Angeles Rams   c. Detroit Lions

Answers: 41-a, 42-c, 43-a, 44-b, 45-c, 46-c, 47-c, 48-a, 49-a, 50-b

51. After several allegations of cheating, what nickname was given to the New England Patriots?

   a. New England Cheaters   b. New England Losers   c. Cheatriots

52. In 1977, which team was known as the 'Gritz Blitz?'

   a. Atlanta Falcons   b. Seattle Seahawks   c. Chicago Bears

53. Which NFL team is Gang Green?

   a. Philadelphia Eagles   b. Green Bay Packers   c. New York Jets

54. What was the nickname for Coach Marty Schottenheimer's strategy?

   a. Schotty Ball   b. Marty Ball   c. MS Ball

55. Which NFL team is also known as the 'Iggles?'

   a. Philadelphia Eagles   b. Baltimore Ravens   c. Miami Dolphins

56. Who is known as the Ageless Wonder?

   a. Brett Favre   b. Darrell Green   c. Aaron Rogers

57. Who is known as Big Ben?

   a. Ben Roethlisberger   b. Ben Graham   c. Ben Coates

58. What is Edgerrin James nickname?

   a. Eddie   b. Edge   c. Edgie

59. Who has the nickname "Manster," half man, half monster?

   a. Reggie White   b. Odell Beckham Jr   c. Randy White

60. Who is the 'Papa Bear?'

   a. George Halas   b. Vince Lombardi   c. Don Shula

Answers: 51-c, 52-a, 53-c, 54-b, 55-a, 56-b, 57-a, 58-b, 59-c, 60-a

61. Who was known as "The Duke" before his passing?

    a. Wellington Mara   b. Drew Brees c. Reggie White

62. Which head coach had a 'classroom approach' to football?

    a. Don Shula   b. Jim Harbaugh   c. Paul Brown

63. Who was the only head coach to win three Super Bowls with three different quarterbacks?

    a. Bill Belichick   b. Joe Gibbs c. Bill Parcells

64. Which coach was associated with the Chicago Bears from the team's inception to his death in 1983?

    a. Vince Lombardi   b. George Halas   c. John Madden

65. Which head coach revitalized the Dallas Cowboys in the 1990s?

    a. Jimmy Johnson   b. Mike Tomlin   c. John Grudden

66. Which head coach said "They call it coaching, but it is teaching"?

    a. Bill Walsh   b. Ed Reid c. Vince Lombardi

67. Which NFL coach put his name on a video game in 1990?

    a. Clark Hunt   b. John Madden   c. Jim Irsay

68. Which head coach turned the New York Jets into a 1-16 team into a 9-7 team in one year?

    a. Bill Parcells   b. Jimmy Johnson   c. Bill Belichick

69. Which head coach has the nickname "The Genius?"

    a. Bill Walsh   b. Bill Parcells   c. Bill Belichick

70. Who is the only head coach to have a perfect, 17-0 season?

    a. Bill Belichick b. Mike Tomlin c. Don Shula

Answers: 61-a, 62-c, 63-b, 64-b, 65-a, 66-c, 67-b, 68-a, 69-a, 70-c

DID YOU KNOW?

1. Former NFL quarterback Tim Tebow has suffered from dyslexia from childhood.

2. More serious injuries are reported at the college football level than in the NFL.

3. Average game attendance for an NFL day is about 66,000 people.

4. The Dallas Cowboys cheerleading squad was originally known as the CowBelles.

5. The shortest player in the NFL was Jack Shapiro, who played for the Staten Island Stapeltons 1929. He stood 5'1" and weighed 119lbs.

6. Roughly three quarters of all NFL players file for bankruptcy within three years of retirement.

7. The leather for official NFL footballs comes from Kansas, Ohio, and Nebraska.

8. Derrick Coleman was the first legally Deaf offensive player in the NFL.

9. The Super Bowl uses Roam numerals to identify itself, except for Super Bowl 50. Marketing experts did not like the look of the single "L" standing for 50.

10. Super Bowl LV (55) marks the first time a playing team has home field advantage.

"When you're GOOD at something, you'll tell everyone. When you're GREAT at something, they'll tell you."- Walter Payton

If you enjoy this book, we have a very modest request: *please take a few seconds to leave us a review on this book's Amazon product page.*

You can't imagine how pleased we are for the support, and we are doing our *best* to deliver you the best books. We wish you only the best
Sincerely,
Brainy Tiger Team

XII. Random

1. How many pounds is the Lombardi Trophy?

   a. 3 pounds b. 5 pounds c. 7 pounds

2. Which NFL team holds the tie for most Superbowl wins *and* losses?

   a. New England Patriots b. Las Vegas Raiders c. Seattle Seahawks

3. In what year was there a blackout during the Super Bowl?

   a. 2013 b. 2017 c. 2021

4. What team played, but lost, four Super Bowls in the early 1990s?

   a. New York Giants b. Detroit Lions c. Buffalo Bills

5. What Grammy award-winning Motown singer tried out for the Detroit Lions in 1970?

   a. Marvin Gaye b. Michael Jackson c. James Brown

6. When was the National Anthem included in NFL kickoff?

   a. 1910 b. 1938 c. 1942

7. What did Chad Johnson change his name to in 2008?

   a. Chad 'Ochocinco' b. Chad the Monster c. Chad Chadster

8. What are the two conferences of the NFL?

   a. North and South b. East and West c. NFC and AFC

9. What is a BYE week?

   a. When a team waves as they walk off the field

   b. When a team has a week off

   c. When a team travels

10. Which NFL team was originally owned by the family who owned the high-end store Nordstrom's?

   a. San Diego Chargers b. San Francisco 49ers c. Seattle Seahawks

Answers: 1-c, 2-a, 3-b, 4-c, 5-a, 6-c, 7-a, 8-c, 9-b, 10-c

11. Which team is named after the date they were founded?

    a. New Orleans Saints b. Chicago Bears c. Carolina Panthers

12. How many teams play in the NFL?

    a. 42   b. 32 c. 22

13. Where did the Oakland Raiders move in 2020?

    a. New York   b. Oakland   c. Las Vegas

14. Which two teams always play on Thanksgiving?

    a. Dallas Cowboys and Detroit Lions b. Tampa Bay Buccaneers and Detroit Lions c. Dallas Cowboys and Carolina Panthers

15. What is the touchdown part of the field called?

    a. The Goal Zone b. The Score Zone c. The End Zone

16. Which of these is *not* a position in the NFL?

    a. Nickelback   b. Full Back   c. Penny Back

17. How long is halftime in the NFL?

    a. 12 minutes   b. 15 minutes   c. 20 minutes

18. What is a 'red flag?'

    a. Coach objects to a play b. Player objects to a play c. Ref stops play

19. What color is the official NFL football?

    a. Black b. navy blue   c. leather brown

20. Where are the NFL headquarters?

    a. New York City b. Houston c. St. Louis

Answers: 11-a, 12-b, 13-c, 14-a, 15-c, 16-c, 17-a, 18-a, 19-c, 20-a

21. How many NFL stadiums still use natural grass?

   a. 15   b. 17   c. 19

22. In what year did Monday Night Football begin?

   a. 1970   b. 1975   c. 1980

23. Who played during the first ever Monday Night Football game?

   a. Cleveland Browns and New York Jets   b. Cleveland Browns and Cincinnati Bengals   c. New York Jets and Kansas City Chiefs

24. Where is the Football Hall of Fame?

   a. Canton, Ohio   b. Jersey City, New Jersey   C. Provo, Utah

25. What are the colors on the official NFL shield?

   a. Red, white, green   b. red, blue, grey   c. red, white, blue

26. Who won the first Super Bowl?

   a. Green Bay Packers   b. Chicago Bears   c. Dallas Cowboys

27. Who won the first NFL Most Valuable Player Award?

   a. Coach Mike Tomlin   b. Bart Starr   c. Walter Camp

28. In what year did a marching band first play at half time?

   a. 1927   b. 1917   c. 1907

29. When did the NFL introduce 'throwback uniforms?'

   a. 1981   b. 1991   c. 2001

30. Which NFL legend helped found the NFL in 1920, owned and coached a team at the same time, coached and played for the team at the same time, and *also* played Major League Baseball for the New York Yankees?

   a. Pat O'Shaunessey   b. Paddy Driscoll   c. George Halas

Answers: 21-a, 22-c, 23-a, 24-c, 25-a, 26-b, 27-c, 28-b, 29-c, 30-c

31. Who is the only quarterback in the NFL to have thrown over 5,000 yards in one season in both college and the pros?

    a. Tom Brady   b. Dan Marino   c. Patrick Mahomes

32. Which NFL team is known as The Dirty Birds?

    a. Atlanta Falcons b. Philadelphia Eagles c. Seattle Seahawks

33. Which NFL team is the most valuable?

    a. New York Jets b. Dallas Cowboys c. Seattle Seahawks

34. How many footballs are used in an NFL game?

    a. 36   b. 46   c. 56

35. Which state does NOT have three NFL teams?

    a. California   b. Washington c. Florida

36. How many states do not have any NFL teams?

    a. 25   b. 27   c. 29

37. NFL football was created from which two sports?

    a. handball and soccer b. soccer and volleyball   c. soccer and rugby

38. Which NFL player also won Dancing With The Stars?

    a. Emmitt Smith   b. Jerry Rice   c. Terry Bradshaw

39. Where is the NFL Pro Bowl played?

    a. Disneyland   b. Disneyworld c. Hawaii

40. How many NFL games have had a spread of 20 or more points?

    a. 5   b. 11   c. 16

Answers: 31-c, 32-a, 33-b, 34-a, 35-b, 36-b, 37-c, 38-a, 39-c, 40-b

41. What is L.A. Rams' Devlin Hodges hidden talent?

    a. tap dancing   b. tight rope walking   c. duck calling

42. Which player first had his number retired by multiple teams?

    a. Deion Sanders   b. Tom Brady   c. Reggie White

43. In 2017, which NFL player was voted the best looking in the league?

    a. Joe Flacco   b. Matt Ryan   c. Tom Brady

44. Why was only one NFL game was played on a Wednesday?

    a. team illness   b. re-scheduled due to a blizzard   c. fire at the stadium

45. Who was the first player in NFL history to be named MVP unanimously?

    a. Lamar Jackson   b. Tom Brady   c. Peyton Manning

46. In 1973, who was the first player to score two safeties in a single game?

    a. Eric Dickerson   b. Marshall Faulk   c. Fred Dryer

47. Which quarterback holds the record for most interceptions thrown?

    a. Brett Favre   b. Peyton Manning   c. Joe Flacco

48. Which team won Super Bowl X?

    a. Green Bay Packers   b. Chicago Bears   c. Pittsburgh Steelers

49. Who won Super Bowl XXV?

    a. New York Giants   b. New York Jets   c. Buffalo Bills

50. Who was the first team in the NFL to win a record 6 Super Bowls?

    a. Baltimore Ravens   b. Pittsburgh Steelers   c. Cleveland Browns

Answers: 41-c, 42-c, 43-a, 44-b, 45-b, 46-c, 47-a, 48-c, 49-a, 50-b

51. In 2014, which kicker recovered his own on side kick?

    a. Matt Bryant   b. Pat McAfee   c. Josh Brown

52. Who is the only quarterback to have Super Bowl wins in three different decades?

    a. Tom Brady   b. Ben Roethlisberger   c. Brett Favre

53. How many seasons did Ray Lewis wait between his Super Bowl wins with the Baltimore Ravens?

    a. 8 b. 12 c. 14

54. Which NFL coach has the most Super Bowl appearances, with 12?

    a. Bill Belichick   b. Mike Tomlin   c. Bill Parcells

55. Which NFL team scored the most points in one Super Bowl?

    a. New England Patriots b. San Francisco 49ers c. Green Bay Packers

56. Which NFL team had the most consecutive losing seasons?

    a. Tampa Bay Buccaneers b. Jacksonville Jaguars c. Detroit Lions

57. Which NFL team had the most ties in one season?

    a. Pittsburgh Steelers   b. Chicago Bears   c. Green Bay Packers

58. Which NFL team scored the most touchdowns in a single season (it was 2013)?

    a. Indianapolis Colts   b. Houston Texans   c. Denver Broncos

59. Which NFL team had the most successful two-point conversions in a single season (2015)?

    a. Dallas Cowboys b. Jacksonville Jaguars c. Pittsburgh Steelers

60. Which team scored the most field goals in one season (2011)?

    a. New York Jets b. San Francisco 49ers c. Buffalo Bills

Answers: 51-b, 52-a, 53-b, 54-a, 55-b, 56-a, 57-b, 58-c, 59-c, 60-b

61. What does the abbreviation PAT stand for?

    a.   player after travel b. play after touchdown c. point after touchdown

62. What does a fair catch signal?

    a.   receiver cannot be hit or run after a punt   b. a ref signal c. coach play

63. What is the 'coffin corner?'

    a.   The area between the five yead line and the end zone

    b.   The area around the quarter back

    c.   The area around the receiver

64. What is a down?

    a.   penalty   b. incomplete pass   c. period of football play

65. What is 'clipping?'

    a.   tackling the below the knees b. grabbing the arms c. interference

66. How many points is a safety worth?

    a.   1   b. 2   c. 3

67. How many points is a field goal worth?

    a.   1   b. 2   c. 3

68. What is the common name for the 'split end?'

    a.   Quarterback   b. Cornerback c. Wide Receiver

69. What is the term for 'advancing the ball by running, not passing?'

    a.   rushing b. ramming   c. robbing

70. What is another name for a 'down lineman?'

    a.   lineman who fell   b. lineman who counts downs   c. a defensive lineman

Answers: 61-c, 62-a, 63-a, 64-c, 65-a, 66-b, 67-c, 68-c, 69-a, 70-c

71. What is the quarterback doing when he is 'scrambling?'

    a. avoiding the defense   b. looking for a receiver   c. play calling

72. What is a 'gap?'

    a. defensive play b. a time out   c. an opening for a receiver

73. What is a 'hail Mary?'

    a. a team slogan b. a long hopeful pass   c. a team prayer

74. What is the term for a defensive player leaving his position last minute?

    a. power play   b. blitz   c. surprise move

75. What is a series of plays when the offense has the ball?

    a. drive   b. power play   c. O-go

76. What is the term for a tight spin on a football?

    a. turn   b. spiral   c. twist

77. Who doesn't play in the wildcat formation?

    a. quarterback   b. running back   c. wide receiver

78. When the quarterback calls a play at the line of scrimmage, what is he calling?

    a. an audible   b. a change play   c. player's choice

79. When both teams commit a foul on the same play, what does the ref call?

    a. double pens   b. two rules   c. double foul

80. Which group does the guard belong to?

    a. O line   b. D line   c. Special Teams

Answers: 71-a, 72-c, 73-b, 74-b, 75-a, 76-b, 77-a, 78-a, 79-c, 80-a

81. What was Sammy Baugh's nickname?

    a. Super   b. Slingin'   c. Sensational

82. What was the NFL's big experiment in 1992?

    a. adding an extra player on the field

    b. b. adding time on the clock

    c. c. adding another BYE week

83. Where was the coldest Super Bowl on record played?

    a. Buffalo, New York b. Chicago, Illinois c. New Orleans, Louisiana

84. What sport did football surpass to be labeled "America's Pastime?"

    a. baseball   b. tennis   c. hockey

85. When was the home field advantage awarded for the post season?

    a. 1970   b. 1975   c. 1980

86. How many consecutive games did Brett Favre play?

    a. 177   b. 277   c. 377

87. Which is the only team that started 0-4, but eventually made the playoffs?

    a. 1982 Jets   b. 1982 Chiefs c. 1982 Chargers

88. About what percentage of instant replays are overturned?

    a. 15%   b. 25%   c. 35%

89. Which NFL coach is mentioned in an Eminem song?

    a. George Clark   b. Bill Edwards   c. Marty Schottenheimer

90. Which NFL team has the smallest television market in America?

    a. Las Vegas Raiders   b. Kansas City Chiefs   c. Green Bay Packers

Answers: 81-b, 82-c, 83-c, 84-a, 85-b, 86-b, 87-c, 88-c, 89-c, 90-c

DID YOU KNOW?

1. The Steelers, who currently do not have cheerleaders, were the first team to have cheerleaders at home games. They were called Steelerettes.

2. Film from the first Super Bowl in 1967 exists, but because of a legal battle over rights to royalties, it is not available for viewing.

3. The "G" on the Green Bay Packers helmet does not stand for Green Bay, rather it stands for Greatness.

4. Aside from Thanksgiving, Super Bowl Sunday is the day in which the most food is consumed in the United States.

5. The Denver Broncos were named after a small minor league baseball team with the same name.

6. The New England Patriots is the only team in the NFL with a human mascot.

7. The first Super Bowl was played in Los Angeles, CA.

8. The New England Patriots and the Pittsburgh Steelers are tied with the most Super Bowl wins, with 6 a piece.

9. Justin Tucker, of the Baltimore Ravens, is a classically trained singer who has performed with the Baltimore Symphony Orchestra.

10. Jersey swapping has become a tradition in the NFL, with players exchanging jerseys with friends on opposing teams after each game.

"Winning isn't getting ahead of others, it's getting ahead of yourself." –Roger Staubaugh

FIVE SHORT AND AMAZING NFL STORIES

The Greatest Stadium in the NFL:

Consistently rated the best stadium in all of the NFL, Lambeau Field (named for Earl 'Curly' Lambeau, a co-founder of the Green Bay Packers) in Green Bay, Wisconsin, is a delight for both players and fans. Formerly called "City Stadium,' the wrap-around seating gives all fans great views of the field. The newly invented SportGrass (1997), a hybrid version of Astroturf, implants real grass into a recyclable surface below the field to give the players the best of both live grass and a bouncy, synthetic surface. SportGrass also resists freezing conditions in a particularly cold part of the country.
Lambeau Field is open air, wrap-around stadium built in 1957. Green Bay Wisconsin, is one of the coldest parts of the United States, so this football field has been nicknamed The Frozen Tundra. When the old field was to be replaced by SportGrass, the old field was removed and packed into small boxes and made into keepsakes, which were then sold to fans to raise money for the new field. This is one team that involves its fans in most major team decisions and honors their fans as a part of the team. Green Bay, Wisconsin, really IS the Packers. Green Bay fans are also known as "Cheeseheads" and wear

hats with plastic wedges of cheddar cheese on them. With pride!

Unlike many other NFL stadiums, Lambeau Field has never accepted money from a corporate sponsor. Fans want the name LAMBEAU to remain on their stadium, with good reason; Curly Lambeau co-founded the team in 1919, long before the NFL officially existed and local professional teams played each other in a far more disorganized manner. The Lambeau name is a piece of Green Bay history, and Packers fans fiercely honor their football history.

One of Lambeau Field's greatest moments was The Ice Bowl. The Superbowl of 1967 was played at Lambeau Field, and the weather was harsh. The Green Bay Packers played the Dallas Cowboys on a frigid December 31st. 50,000 fans were in attendance. However, their faces were obscured on the television screens due to their visible breaths from the cold. At game time, the temperature was 13 degrees F *below 0.* The Green Bay Packers came out on top, beating the Dallas Cowboys 21-17. That win was their third straight NFL Championship. It is no wonder Packers fans are so very loyal. Lambeau Field has several nicknames, such as "The House That Lombardi Built" and "Titletown, USA." The stadium sits on the banks of Green Bay, at 1285 Lombardi Avenue. Lambeau Field seats over 81,000 fans, after several expansion projects took it from 50,000 seats. Lambeau Field is the 5th oldest continually operating NFL stadium in the country.

In a classy nod to their history, the Green Bay Packers play two or three games a season in their original City Stadium, holding far fewer fans but many more memories. The Packers do this to pay homage to the great players who wore green and gold before them.

The Manning Dynasty:

Archie Manning was a tall, lean, Quarterback who played mainly for the New Orleans Saints. Born in 1949 in Mississippi, he was heavily involved in school sports. Archie also excelled in baseball, and professional baseball teams sought out his talent four times before Archie committed to playing football as a career. After attending the University of Mississippi, where his performance on the field earned him the title of "Southeastern Conference Quarterback of the Quarter Year 1950-1975," Archie went onto play for the New Orleans Saints from 1971-1982. Archie married Olivia Williams, and together they had three sons: Cooper, Peyton, and Eli. All three were outstanding high school football players. Cooper was unable to pursue a career playing football due to a spinal condition. Peyton, however, was a shooting star.

Peyton Manning played for the University of Tennessee and was then drafted #1 overall in the 1998 draft to play for the Indianapolis Colts. Peyton led the failing team to eight division championships, two AFC championships, and a Superbowl title (2006).

Peyton suffered a severe neck injury that required surgery so intense he was sidelined for the entire 2011 season. Many wondered if Peyton's career was over. The Colts cut him from their roster.

The Denver Broncos believed Peyton Manning could recover and rise to the level of performance he had with the Colts--and he did. Peyton was the quarterback for the Denver Broncos from 2012 until 2015, and he led them to two AFC championships and a Superbowl (Broncos over Panthers, 24-10) in 2016. The following week, Peyton Manning announced his retirement from professional football.

Eli Manning, the youngest Manning brother, was born in New Orleans in 1981 and was a Quarterback like his brother and father. Eli attended the University of Mississippi (aka Ole Miss) like his father. Like his brother, he was drafted #1 overall in 2004 by the New York Giants. Eli remained their starting Quarterback until 2019, when he announced his retirement. While the 'general' of the Giants offense, Eli led the team to two Superbowl victories, notably in 2008 against the New England Patriots. Until the evening of the Superbowl, the Patriots had won every regular-season game. IN 2011 there was a 'rematch' of that Superbowl, where Eli and the New York Giants were once again victorious over the New England Patriots. Eli was voted the Most Valued Player in both Super Bowls and was awarded the game football.

Remember Cooper Manning, the oldest Manning brother who had a promising football career ahead of him but was sidelined with a chronic spine condition? He had a son in 2005. As of 2021, Cooper's son is a star high school football player named Arch...after his grandfather. In his freshman year in high school, Arch was the starting quarterback for the Isadore Newmann High School football team in New Orleans, Louisiana. In his sophomore year's first varsity game, Arch threw for two touchdowns and rushed for two more. There is obviously college chatter about Arch, but his family has kept him away from the media. For now.

Brothers in Arms--Siblings in the NFL:

To date, there have been 29 sets of siblings in the NFL, and a few have been twins. The most famous were the Manning brothers; although both being quarterbacks, they were never on the field at the same time. One set of NFL twins were coaches, Rob and Rex Ryan. Rex Ryan was the head coach for the New York Jets from 2009-2014, and Rob Ryan was a defensive coach (an assistant coach position) for many teams, most notably for the New England Patriots, from 2000-2003. Rob Ryan was on staff with the New England Patriots when they won Super Bowls 36 and 37. Another set of twin coaches are Jim and John Harbough. Jim coaches the San Francisco 49ers, and John coaches the Baltimore Orioles.

Some better-known player siblings are Ronde and Tiki Barber, who played for the Tampa Bay Buccaneers and the New York Giants, respectively. The Watt brothers, JJ, Derek, and TJ, played for the Houston Texans, San Diego Chargers, and Pittsburgh Steelers. Another trio of football-playing brothers is Dan, Chris, and Rob Gronkowski, who played for the Cleveland Browns, the Denver Broncos, and the New England Patriots.

Then there is the special case of the Matthews brothers. Born into an NFL family boasting seven players over four generations, both Clay Matthews Jr and Bruce Matthews played football for the University of Southern California before entering the NFL draft. Both brothers were drafted in the first round of their draft classes (1978 and 1983). Clay Jr played for Cleveland Browns and Atlanta Falcons, while Bruce played for the Oilers/Titans franchise. In both 1988 and 1989, they were the only brothers ever selected to play in the Pro Bowl together in Honolulu, Hawaii.

Two of Bruce's four boys were also NFL players; Jake and Kevin. Clay Jr.'s son Clay III was also an NFL player. In what could be the most interesting twist of families in the NFL, Jake, an Atlanta Falcon, defeated his cousin Clay III and his team, the Green Bay Packers, to advance to the Super Bowl.

The Rise of Tom Brady:

Thomas Brady Jr. was born on August 3, 1977, in San Mateo, California. Brady was equally interested in baseball and football; upon high school graduation, Brady was offered a professional baseball contract from the Montreal Expos. Brady was determined to play football and declined the contract. Eventually, Brady attended the University of Michigan. After sitting out most of his first two years, he led the Michigan Wolverines to Citrus Bowl, and Orange Bowl wins in his junior and senior years.

However, Brady did not impress NFL scouts at the 'combine,' a retreat for recent football-playing college graduates. While there, players are scores on many physical attributes and given a scorecard; Brady's was lacking in most categories. In the 2000 draft, Brady was the 7th quarterback chosen and the 199th player chosen overall.

Brady's potential in professional football was not obvious in 1999.

However, Tom Brady did have a reputation for possessing an outstanding work ethic and 'pocket intelligence.' He could stand with the ball at the beginning of the play and read the field with incredible accuracy, predicting how each player would move. This fierce attention to detail and ability to 'read' the field quickly helped Brady grow into his professional football career. During Brady's rookie year with the New England Patriots, he was the backup quarterback for Drew Bledsoe. Bledsoe took an incredibly hard hit from New York Jets player Mo Jackson, which resulted in a concussion as well as internal bleeding. Tom Brady had to step in as Drew

Bledsoe was taken to a local hospital for treatment (when Bledsoe could not recall the word 'left,' the team doctors knew he needed emergency attention; ultimately, he came close to death in surgery but returned to the NFL with the Buffalo Bills and Dallas Cowboys, and then retired in 2007).

As of 2021, Brady has started 344 games in 20 seasons with the New England Patriots and one with the Tampa Bay Buccaneers. He has a combined 264 wins (regular and postseason), and is the winningest quarterback in NFL history. He appeared in ten Super Bowls and has seven Superbowl rings. Tom Brady holds almost every quarterback record in the NFL, including passing yards, completions, and touchdowns. With the longevity of his career (despite missing almost the entire 2003 season due to a knee injury) also comes age-related records: Tom Brady is the oldest player in the NFL to play in and win a Superbowl (age 43), and be named league Most Valuable Player at age 40. On many lists, Tom Brady is cited as the number 1 player in NFL history. In many football circles, he is known simply as The GOAT: Greatest Of All Time.

The Greatest Superbowl Comeback (2017):

On February 5th, 2017, at NRG Stadium in Houston, Texas, the New England Patriots and the Atlanta Falcons met to compete in the Superbowl. The Patriots were heavily favored. The first quarter ended scoreless on both sides of the ball; the Falcons turned up the heat in the second quarter, and by halftime, the score was 21-3, with the Atlanta Falcons in the lead.

No team had ever come back from an 18-point deficit at halftime at a Superbowl. Ever.

No one knows what happened during halftime in that locker room. Lady Gaga played a halftime show that got the crowd on its feet, and Atlanta fans were convinced the Superbowl was theirs.

But they were wrong.

New England trailed for all but the final two minutes of the game. When the two-minute warning came in the fourth quarter, they were still down by eight points. Eight points are difficult to make in two minutes! But, one thing Tom Brady and the New England Patriots always had was faith in the fourth-quarter comeback. They were masters of the come-from-behind victory, and the next one hundred and twenty seconds played out like a Hollywood script ending. The Patriots *did* score a touchdown and completed the two-point conversion, which tied the game and forced an overtime meeting for the first time in Super Bowl-era history.

The New England Patriots won the coin toss and chose to receive the football. They marched down the field full of confidence. They ran the football into the Atlanta Falcons end zone from the one-yard line, and the game ended with a score of 34-28. This was the outcome, and even though, statistically, the Atlanta Falcons had over a 99% chance of winning after the third quarter. That proves "Nothing Is Impossible."

"It's not the SIZE of the dog in the fight, but the size of the FIGHT in the dog". --**Archie Griffin**

If you enjoy this book, we have a very modest request: *please take a few seconds to leave us a review on this book's Amazon product page.*

You can't imagine how pleased we are for the support, and we are doing our *best* to deliver you the best books.
We wish you only the best
Sincerely,
Brainy Tiger Team

Made in the USA
Coppell, TX
24 November 2021

66252452R00063